GAME,
SET
AND
MATCH

GAME, SET AND MATCH

SECRET WEAPONS
OF THE WORLD'S
TOP TENNIS PLAYERS

MARK HODGKINSON

BLOOMSBURY
LONDON • NEW DELHI • NEW YORK • SYDNEY

Bloomsbury Sport
An imprint of Bloomsbury Publishing Plc

50 Bedford Square   1385 Broadway
London   New York
WC1B 3DP   NY 10018
UK   USA

www.bloomsbury.com

BLOOMSBURY and the Diana logo are trademarks of Bloomsbury Publishing Plc

First published 2015

British Library Cataloguing-in-Publication Data
A catalogue record for this book is available from the British Library.

Library of Congress Cataloguing-in-Publication data has been applied for.

ISBN:
HB: 978-1-4729-0577-2
PB   978-1-4729-2262-5
ePDF: 978-1-4729-2147-5
ePub: 978-1-4729-2146-8

2 4 6 8 10 9 7 5 3 1

Typeset in Haarlemmer MT by Gridlock-design
Printed and bound in the U.S.A. by Thomson-Shore Inc., Dexter, Michigan

To find out more about our authors and books visit www.bloomsbury.com. Here you will find
extracts, author interviews, details of forthcoming events and the option to sign up for our
newsletters.

Dedication
For Amy, Molly and Rosie.

Acknowledgements

This book wouldn't have been possible without the generosity of the world's finest players and coaches – and the assistance of Roger Federer's mother. They were generous with their time and also with their insights – from the first interviewee, Anna Kournikova, to the last, they were very happy to share their secrets. I'm also extremely grateful to all those who facilitated the interviews that led to the tips on these pages, including the communications staff of the men's and women's tours, and the players' management teams (most of the tips collected here first appeared on TheTennisSpace.com). Huge thanks also to my friend and colleague in the tennis media, Simon Cambers, who conducted a number of the interviews that appear in this book, as well as offering ideas and advice along the way. I'm indebted to Charlotte Croft, Sarah Cole and the rest of the fabulous team at Bloomsbury. And also to David Luxton and Rebecca Winfield of David Luxton Associates – this project wouldn't have gone anywhere without their energy and direction.

Contents

INTRODUCTION

Whatever your standard, whatever your age, if you love tennis there is no better way to improve your game than by learning the secrets of the world's greatest players and coaches. *Game, Set and Match* is an unprecedented collection of tips from the world's superstars, who have given advice from inside the professional game, based on their experiences in the white heat of competition on the sport's biggest stages – and now you can use those secrets at your club or at the local courts.

A veritable Who's Who of players and coaches give you their insight and experience about a part of the game – whether technical, physical or mental – for which they have the greatest expertise. Among many others, Andy Murray explains how to hit a drop shot, while Maria Sharapova talks mental toughness, Grigor Dimitrov has tips on hitting tweeners, Eugenie Bouchard on playing on grass, and Gael Monfils on being flexible, while Boris Becker passes on his thoughts on hitting a diving-volley, Chris Evert gives advice on how to deal with nerves, and there's no greater expert than Pete Sampras on the subjects of slam-dunk smashes and disguising your serve. Celebrated during her career for her inside-out forehand, Steffi Graf explains how to play the shot that helped her to win so many grand slam titles, while Milos Raonic, who arguably has the greatest serve of his generation, gives advice on how to hit an ace. Among the other leading coaches to have shared their secrets is Patrick Mouratoglou, who has worked with Serena Williams, and Paul Annacone, who has collaborated with Roger Federer, Pete Sampras, Tim Henman and Sloane Stephens. There's also advice from Rafa Nadal's uncle and coach Toni, from Nick Bollettieri, who has coached ten players who have been the world No. 1, and from Marian Vajda, who guided Novak Djokovic to multiple slam titles. Federer's mother, Lynette, and Ana Ivanovic are among those giving you guidance on being a better tennis parent. Andy Murray's mother, Judy, and Serena and Venus Williams' father, Richard, also pass on their thoughts, as does Gil Reyes, the physical trainer who was so instrumental in the success of Andre Agassi. Do you want to look stylish on court? Venus Williams, who is a clothes designer as well as a multiple grand slam champion, has shared her expertise. Her sister Serena, arguably the greatest female player of all time, has some advice for ambitious juniors.

Covering almost every aspect of the game about which you may wish to enquire, and many others you had probably never thought of, *Game, Set and Match* is a must-have dip-in reference work for all tennis aficionados. I hope you will enjoy it, and benefit from the advice offered.

THE TECHNICAL GAME

SERVING

Pete Sampras, winner of 14 grand slam singles titles,
on 'HOW TO DISGUISE YOUR SERVE' ...

Practise having the same ball toss for all serves: 'I didn't have the fastest serve, but I did have the best, and the disguise helped. There's no point serving fast if your opponent knows where the ball is going, that's worthless. If you can have your opponent guessing, that's worth a lot. People used to say to me, "I just couldn't read your serve." If your body shape is always the same, no matter what serve you're hitting, and your service motion and the position of your racket are always the same too, your opponent is going to find it very difficult to read you. It's all about your hand, your wrist and your grip. It's not easy, so the earlier you start practising disguise the better. I did it from a very early age, as a kid, and so that went into my muscles, and my muscles had those memories. That's why I was able to do that as an adult.'

Try this drill: 'As a kid, my coach would make me do this drill where he would only tell me after I had tossed the ball where he wanted me to hit it. He would shout "out wide" or "down the middle" or he would ask me to *handcuff the opponent with a body serve. That was great as it meant that my toss was always the same, and I didn't know myself where I was going to hit it until right until the last moment. You can have some fun with this, waiting until as late as possible before being told where to hit the ball. If you really want to improve your disguise, do this for hours and hours.'

Improve your accuracy: 'If you can hit your spots, you're going to cause problems for your opponents.'

Don't get hung up on one serve – use as much variety as possible: 'I think many players get fixated on going for the same spot, and that makes them too predictable, so hit all the serves you can, whether that's out wide, down the "T" or to the body. And learn to hit all the spins. Mix it up. Of course, I was able to hit the ball hard. But it was mixing it up, and disguising all those serves, that gave me a better package.'

Milos Raonic, who can serve at 155mph, and played in his first grand slam semi-final at 2014 Wimbledon, on 'HOW TO HIT AN ACE' ...

Accuracy is the number one thing: 'If you hit the line, it doesn't matter whether it's at 140mph or 120mph, it's hard for someone to get it back. I don't necessarily aim to hit the line but pretty close to it. I aim about an inch or two inside the line. So I give myself some margin.'

You need variety: 'You have to be able to hit different serves, because if you can only hit the line with one serve, your opponent can cheat that way and cover that side. Guys move and return too well nowadays. So you have to be able to hit all the serves and hit them well.' Change it up based on what has been happening during the match, and where your opponent is standing.

Improve your accuracy with drills on the practice court – you have to keep hitting a certain serve until you're getting at least six out of ten: 'You can usually feel whether you're serving well or whether you need to do some work to sharpen it.'

Never expect to serve an ace – you must be prepared to play another shot: 'I always expect the ball to come back. If it doesn't come back, it's a good thing, but you must be prepared for the ball to be returned. You can never think, "If I hit that there, it's not coming back."'

However, if you do hit an ace, recognise that it will help you psychologically: 'Of course, it gives you freedom, as you don't have to play the point. But it's more what it does to the other guy. It keeps them guessing, it keeps them feeling pressure as it makes them think that they need to hold serve. I feel that, if I do get ahead a break, more often than not I will hold out the rest of the set. So me breaking them can mean the end of the set. That pressure helps me out too.'

Sabine Lisicki, a former Wimbledon finalist who has held the record for the fastest serve in the women's game,
on 'HOW TO SERVE AT 131MPH' ...

The key to hitting a fast serve is rhythm: 'Without rhythm, you will struggle. To get rhythm on your serve, you need to spend some time on the practice court – when you've got it you can stand there on the baseline, just toss the ball up and hit it as hard as you can. It's a nice thing knowing that you can serve at 131mph – it's great to have the record – but I know it's all about the rhythm. I've hit thousands and thousands of serves, and you're going to have to as well if you want to get a faster serve.'

Don't be fooled into thinking that power is everything, and that all you have to do is hit the ball as hard as possible: 'You also need to think about where you're directing the ball. There's no point hitting it at full power towards your opponent's racket as then it's going to come right back at you just as fast. I mix it up, and don't always hit my first serves at full power. Sometimes it's not possible anyway, because of the wind, but even in good conditions I don't always go for full power. You want to keep your opponent guessing.'

Sam Groth, who holds the world record for the fastest recorded serve,
on 'HOW TO SERVE AT 163MPH' ...

Hit it flat down the 'T': 'The flatter serves are the quick ones. If you're going to hit a big one, you take all the spin off as the spin slows the ball down.

With spin, the ball is going to move in the air a bit more – it's going to move in shape – and so your serve isn't going to fly as quickly. When I broke the record, it was a full flat slap down the "T". I was playing a tournament in Korea and I knew they were quick conditions. The balls were hard and fast. When I hit that one at 163mph, I had a new ball and I really went for a big serve. My opponent didn't even have time to finish his split-step, and he threw his arms up in the air as if to say, "What could I have done?" I looked up at the screen, but at that stage I was still trying to win the match. It took a few days to get it verified by the ATP. It's a great feeling to be the best in the world at something. It's only one part of tennis but it's something I'm pretty proud of.'

'I used to serve 150, 200 balls a night.'
SAM GROTH

Try to stay relaxed: 'If I try to really wallop the ball, I'm prone to mis-hits, and I end up being all over the shop. I've found that I tend to serve my biggest when I'm relaxed. There are days when I come out and roll my arm over, and I get almost as much power. Everyone's motion and rhythm is going to be different, but generally I would say it's best to have an easy, relaxed service action. Obviously, you're still going to be throwing your arm at the ball, but you don't want to throw yourself off balance, or mess up your swing.'

If you practise your serve enough, it will evolve naturally and you will have an easy, relaxed action: 'I'm from a small town in Australia, and I didn't really have anyone to practise with. I think the older guys thought they were too good for me. From the age of 10 until I was 14, I used to serve 150, 200 balls a night; it was just something I worked on. You see people out there, fiddling about with where their arm should be. But I had hit enough serves over time that it just evolved naturally. If you hit enough of them, you learn how to hit the ball in the box, and you learn how to hit it hard.'

Don't serve at full pace throughout the match – just when you're up in games: 'I tend to go for the really big ones when I'm up in games. You have to remember that when you go for the really big ones, there's less chance of it going in. Maybe at 40-0 or at 40-15, I would look to load up a little bit. I don't really want to be hitting a second serve at 30-all after my big flat one has hit the tape or landed out. It depends on your opponent – if he's not really getting on to my second, I wouldn't be afraid to go for my first a bit more.'

To hit a really big serve, you need the right conditions: 'There are a lot of things that make a difference when it comes to hitting a big serve. It's the balls, the temperature, the humidity, the altitude. On a warm day, the air is lighter. At altitude, the air is lighter. The harder the ball, the quicker it's going to slingshot off your racket. A fluffier ball might sit on your racket a little bit more.'

Sam Stosur, a former US Open champion,
on 'HOW TO HIT THE PERFECT KICK SERVE' ...

Nail down the ball toss: 'To hit a good kick serve it needs to be to the left for a right-hander and, I find, a little bit behind. You don't want the ball to be too far in front of you, too far into the court. If you think of a square, you're moving the racket from the bottom left corner up to the top right.'

Use your whole body: 'You have to have good core strength and the ability to bend. You don't necessarily want to be thinking specifically about bending your back; a lot of it's got to come from the legs as well. Then, you need good rotation through your shoulders.'

Make sure you mix it up: 'The best disguise is being able to hit the serve to any part of the box, off the same ball toss. The easiest spot to hit it to is typically the opponent's backhand and I can usually do that with my eyes closed. But at this level, players can work it out and their backhands are very good, so you do have to work out how to hit it to different spots for the element of surprise. However, while you need to be aware of the need to mix it up, you still don't want to get too far away from what you like to do and the serves you like hitting the most. You've got to back your strength against your opponent's.'

Sabine Lisicki, a former Wimbledon finalist,
on 'HOW TO HIT A BODY SERVE' ...

Accuracy is essential: 'If you miss the body, if you're just out, you're going to be putting the ball right into their hitting-zone.'

Put some power behind the serve, but don't go for so much power that you lose all accuracy: 'I like to serve big, but you also have to place it well, so you need to find a balance between the two. Power and speed isn't everything – body serves work well on all surfaces, not just on the faster surfaces.'

If you hit your opponent, you don't have to apologise: 'If I accidentally hit my opponent I say sorry, but it's up to you.'

Kevin Anderson, who has been ranked in the world's top 20,
on 'HOW TO SERVE DOWN THE "T"' ...

The ball needs to be up at 12 o'clock and it needs to be up high: 'Getting that right is key to this serve.'

Have a very specific target: 'I look between the net strap and the centre line and focus on the spot where I want to land the ball.'

Don't make the mistake of thinking that you always have to hit this serve flat with no spin: 'Mix it up a little bit. Sometimes play with spin, and sometimes play a flatter ball. If you're starting out, and learning how to play this serve, I would suggest putting a little bit of spin on it to control the ball. You definitely don't want to hit this completely flat.'

Pete Sampras, who won seven Wimbledon titles,
on 'HOW TO HAVE A GREAT SECOND SERVE' ...

Have the guts to be aggressive with your second serve: 'I always judge a great server from the second serve. On their day, anyone can serve well and hit aces with their first serve, but if it's off, which sometimes it can be, you want to have a second serve that's offensive and gives you opportunities, not just looking to get the ball in. The key to the second serve is having a technically sound serve, so that under pressure you can go for it. Then it's about having the balls to actually do it.'

Learn to pick your spots: 'You've got to pick your spots on the serve. It's one thing I always felt like I did pretty well. I could mix up my serve, go to the body, to the forehand or backhand.'

Roger Federer and Pete Sampras'
former coach, **Paul Annacone**
on 'HOW TO IMPROVE THE PLACEMENT ON YOUR SERVE' ...

Don't hit too many serves: 'Too many players hit "baskets" of serves. It's great to do this if you are working on rhythm or technique, but if you are looking to get more accurate, it's better to hit fewer serves and to put greater importance on each one. Warm the body, arm and shoulder up – then make every serve count.'

Challenge yourself: 'Grade yourself on each serve between one and ten. I don't believe in tens, but you get the idea. Make sure you put yourself up to a challenge. Set a target for ten serves to different locations, and you have to average at least 7.5. If you don't make it, what's the forfeit? – Push-ups, or sprints, or buying lunch for your coach, which is my favourite.'

Petra Kvitova, a multiple Wimbledon champion,
on 'PRACTISING YOUR SERVE' ...

Don't overdo it on the practice court: 'You don't want to hit so many serves that you start to feel it in your arm and shoulder and then you're not right for the matches. These days, I don't measure it in time, but usually in balls, so I take, say, 60 balls and serve those until I'm happy with how I'm striking the ball.'

Practise the spins as well as the placements.

Goran Ivanisevic, a former Wimbledon champion,
on 'HOW TO IMPROVE YOUR SERVE' ...

Hit more body serves: 'No one serves into their opponent's body any more. It's an unbelievable serve, and I don't why people don't use that shot any more. Maybe they think they're not allowed to. With a body serve, when the guy returns, he doesn't have an angle because the ball is jammed into his body and there's not much he can do. You can give them a slow body serve, and then a fast one – mix it up. People just want to hit ace, ace, ace. They keep on going for the same spots and trying to hit aces. OK, eventually you're going to get your aces, but maybe you've been broken two or three times because you've become so predictable and your opponent knows what you're going to do.'

Don't be afraid to put some pace on your second serve: 'When I hit my second serve slowly, the ball used to go into the bottom of the net. So I thought it was better to hit the ball properly. At least that would give me a 50-50 chance of winning the point.'

Like most players, you probably need to spend more time practising your serve: 'The most important shots in tennis are serve and return. And people don't practise them enough. The serve is a very difficult shot. People think it's easy – that you just throw the ball up, and hit it, and that's it. You need to work hard. Don't just rally balls from the back of the practice court all day.'

> **'No one serves into their opponent's body any more and I don't know why.'**
> GORAN IVANISEVIC

The best way to make service practice fun is to have some cans to aim at: 'I used to practise a lot to improve my accuracy. Practising your serve can be pretty boring, but I used to put cans in the service box and aim at those, trying to improve my accuracy at hitting the corners. If you have a little competition with yourself, you can serve for half an hour, 45 minutes, without even realising it. That's great. But if you're just standing there serving, and there's nothing to aim at, and it's not fun, mentally that's pretty tough.'

Just before a match, practise your serve until it 'clicks in your head': 'When I was preparing for matches, I would serve (it could be for just five minutes or for nearly an hour), and then as soon as it clicked, I would tell myself, "that's enough" and I would stop, as I could only serve worse after that.'

Elina Svitolina, who in 2014 was the highest ranked teenager in women's tennis, on **'HOW TO COPE WHEN YOU ARE SERVING LOTS OF DOUBLE-FAULTS'** ...
Don't rush. Slow down and really think about what you're doing: 'Take your time between points, and between serves. Don't just go from one serve to another without being aware of what you're doing.'

Don't panic – take confidence from the work you've done on your serve on the practice court, and how you have served in previous matches: 'It's important to stay calm in your head, and to think about what you have been doing on the practice court, and what your coach has said to you.'

Recognise that every day can't be perfect – you're going to have some tough days when you serve lots of double-faults. When that happens, don't give up: 'You don't get a perfect day every day. Of course, there will be some days when I will serve ten or more double-faults. But you just have to keep going.'

Ivo Karlovic, who can serve at 156mph,
on 'HOW TO GET THE MOST FROM YOUR SERVE' ...

You need to stay loose: 'On court, you have to be relaxed because if you're not relaxed, your arm will be too stiff and then it won't be as quick.'

Mark Philippoussis, a former Wimbledon and US Open finalist,
on 'HOW TO GET YOUR BALL TOSS RIGHT' ...

Hold the ball on the tips of your fingers: 'You see some kids hold the ball in the palm of their hands, and then when it comes to the moment of release they kind of flick it out. If you hold the ball on the tips of your fingers, that allows you to guide the ball out and up.'

Guide the ball up with a straight arm, as that will give you a consistent toss: 'You see players with a bent arm, and the toss becomes very inconsistent.'

The height of the ball toss depends on your height, and whether you jump into the serve, and how much you jump into the ball: 'Ideally, you want to extend your body as that's how you are going to hit your best serves. It's better to have your ball toss higher than lower. But you don't want to toss the ball so high that you end up hitting the ball when it's on the way down. You want to hit it when it's suspended in the air.'

Don't lower your toss on a windy day. Keep the same toss: 'You look at where the wind is blowing. So if, for example, the wind is blowing from right to left, you toss the ball a little bit to the right so it will move to where you want to hit it. You need to look at any flags around the stadium so you can work out where you're going to toss the ball.'

If you're serving into the sun, you can move along the baseline to get a different angle: 'And, on your second serve, perhaps try hitting the ball a little further back. You've got to change that toss and get out of that sun. After 20 minutes, remember that the sun will have moved, so you will look again at the conditions. Throughout the match, the sun is going to keep moving so you have to see what it's doing and how you're going to react to that.'

Madison Keys, who appeared in her first grand slam semi-final at the 2015 Australian Open, on 'HOW TO TAKE THE STRESS OUT OF SERVING' ...

You should have a go-to serve on both sides: 'These are the serves that you feel most comfortable with. You should have a serve that you hit when it's very tight and you need to make a first serve. For example, I know that my kick serve on the ad side is a serve I feel really comfortable with. So if I'm down a break, and it's 15-30, and I really feel as though I need to get the point started, I'll throw in a kick serve.'

If you're having a bad day with your serve, just take your time and think about the basics – such as the ball toss. But don't start putting extra pressure on yourself to make a serve: 'I just try to think about the very basic things that help me to have a good serve, instead of thinking, "I have to make this serve." If I can get my serve going, the rest of my game just flows, and my service games are a lot less stressful. That allows me to focus more on the returning games, and breaking my opponent.'

Hit baskets and baskets of serves each day: 'That's the key to having a good serve, and that will give you confidence in the shot.'

Mark Philippoussis
on 'HOW TO INTIMIDATE WITH YOUR SERVE' ...

Hit some bombs, or big serves, in the warm-up. And perhaps even try to hit your opponent: 'Let him hear the ball whizzing by, and then smacking hard into the backstop. Then he'll be thinking, "Oh gosh, this guy serves pretty big." And if you hit him, that will intimidate him.'

Serve at 100 per cent from the start: 'I never wanted to just ease into it, as the serve was my weapon. Why would you wait until later in the match before using your weapon? You're letting a guy into the match from the start and that's not a good play.'

Use your own serve to put more pressure on your opponent's delivery: 'If you have a big serve and you're very confident you're going to hold easily, the great thing is you can then take more chances on return. Your opponent knows that if they happen to play one weak service game and get broken, the set will pretty much be over. That counts for a lot. Guys can get tight easily.'

Hitting a lot of aces can be intimidating: 'Your opponent will get frustrated, as he's going to be walking from side to side without hitting the ball and so he hasn't got any rhythm. That's definitely not a good situation for him. And don't forget about body serves. It's actually a very important serve. It's easily forgotten, as people like to serve aces. But you can intimidate with a body serve.'

Sergiy Stakhovsky, who used this tactic to beat Roger Federer at the 2013 Wimbledon Championships, on 'HOW TO SERVE AND VOLLEY' ...

You have to be smarter than your opponent – you have to put doubt and chaos into his game: 'It's very hard to play serve and volley all the time. You also need the ability to stay back on the baseline, as otherwise it's very hard to succeed in today's game. You have to make sure he doesn't know whether you're going to come in or not. You have to mix it up and trick him. And he will make more mistakes.'

If you serve and volley the whole time, be prepared for your opponent to hit the ball at you as hard as he can: 'That's going to be a problem for you, so be ready.'

Sometimes when you serve and volley a lot, that can take your opponent by surprise: ' I used the tactic against Federer; he didn't expect me to do it from the start of the match. He also didn't expect me to keep on doing it.'

You can't ever relax: 'You have to be using your brain the whole time. You need to be thinking, outsmarting your opponent.'

It's hard to recommend serve and volleying with any regularity on clay or on a hard court: 'You can do it on grass. But, on any other surface, when it's so slow, your opponent is going to stand six metres behind the baseline and you're going to have no chance. You probably won't even get the chance to play a volley as he is going to hit the ball right past you.'

Tim Henman, four times a Wimbledon semi-finalist,
on 'WHEN TO SERVE AND VOLLEY' ...

Don't rush your serve: 'You want to hit your serve properly before going to the net. If you execute your serve properly, that will set you up for the first volley. Don't panic and think that you need to get to the net too quickly. Focus on taking your time with your serve and hitting your spot.'

Understand the angle, and cover the return down the line: 'If you're serving out wide, you obviously don't want to move into the middle of the court when you go to the net – you want to move wide to cover the line. Sometimes, your opponent will get the ball across you and hit a winner, and you have to accept that it's just too good a return. But you don't want to be beaten up the line.'

Change your tactics from surface to surface: 'If you're serve and volleying on clay, which is obviously tough to do, it's important to volley behind your opponent and not always hit the ball to the open court. Changing direction on clay is difficult, and the earlier in the match you can volley behind your opponent and force them to change direction, the better. You will sow the seed of doubt that you are not always going to play the ball into the open court, as your opponent probably would have expected you to do that most, if not all, of the time. That will keep your opponent guessing.'

Be careful about coming in behind your second serve: 'It should be a surprise tactic to keep them guessing, but it's not something that I would advise doing a great deal of. I would love to see more people coming to the net, but you have to be realistic about it, and look at the conditions and the athleticism of the players and how hard they hit the ball. If you come to the net, you have to make sure that you're going in after the right ball – otherwise you will be in trouble.'

FOREHAND

Rafa Nadal's uncle and coach, Toni,
on 'HOW TO PLAY A TOPSPIN FOREHAND' ...

You need a good wrist, a fast wrist: 'You need to be able to move the wrist very quickly. Also, the arm needs to be relaxed.'

You need to hit the ball with a lot of speed, as you can only generate a lot of spin if the racket is moving quickly. Make sure you swing through the ball as otherwise you will lose power and speed on the shot: 'The biggest mistake you can make when hitting a topspin forehand is when you move the racket up too quickly. That won't produce a good shot, as you need that forward movement. If all you're doing is moving the racket up, you will get lots of revolutions on the ball, lots of spin, but when the ball bounces on your opponent's side of the court – boom – it will lose all its speed. If you're generating too much spin, sometimes the ball goes a little short; it's not so easy to put the ball deep into your opponent's court.'

Remember that topspin doesn't work as well against taller opponents, or on hard courts with low bounces: 'In this game, there is not only one way to be a good player. When you play against taller opponents – against Juan

Martin del Potro rather than David Ferrer – topspin isn't so effective. It's good at Roland Garros and at other clay-court tournaments, but not always so good on hard courts when the ball doesn't bounce so much.'

Steffi Graf, a winner of 22 grand slam singles titles,
on 'HOW TO RUN AROUND YOUR BACKHAND TO ATTACK WITH YOUR FOREHAND' ...

Use your backhand to create space and time for your forehand: 'My forehand was my strength; it was the shot from which I could generate most pace and power. It allowed me to make progress in the point as I was able to hit it a variety of ways, flat or with spin, and I felt I could not only push my opponent into defensive positions but also finish points when the opportunity was there. My backhand was the shot that I used to create space and time to set up my forehand, and once I took control of the point on my forehand side I attempted to make it difficult for my opponent to find my backhand by working hard with my feet.'

Running around your backhand will send a strong message to your opponent that you are looking to use your strengths and to be offensive: 'It is an important shot at any level of the game, on any surface. It does become a little more difficult to execute on the faster surfaces, but it's still sending out a strong message.'

Recognise your opponent's capabilities: 'If my right-handed opponent has a strong backhand down the line, I would need to be a little more selective when playing the shot as I was exposing so much open court. Also, recognise when your opponent is playing a defensive shot as that is the time to become more active with your feet to try to control the point with your forehand.'

Don't watch your shot: 'Always make the move to recover to the middle of the court after running around your backhand to hit the forehand.'

Give yourself enough space to execute an offensive swing on the forehand: 'Good footwork is the key to a good forehand. Try at all times to have your body moving forward and through the line of the ball towards your target at impact to enhance timing and power.'

The biggest mistake you can make is to get into the habit of only hitting the forehand in one direction: 'Your opponent will quickly work out your patterns. You need to be able to hit a variety of shots from that position so your opponent will feel the need to cover all parts of the court. In an ideal situation, your opponent will feel some panic when they see you dance around to unload on a forehand and will back up in the court to take up a more defensive position. That is when you can do the most damage with your forehand as the angles of the court become available to you.'

You can surprise your opponent if you are willing and able to hit this shot early in the point: 'Players that hit it well are known for having it in their arsenal and their opponents expect it. But, the surprise element is always a big factor if you are willing and able to hit it early in the point when your opponent hasn't settled into the rhythm of the rally. For example, making an aggressive move to return a second serve is a perfect time to surprise your opponent.'

Appreciate that there is a risk playing this shot as you can leave yourself out of position, but you should always be looking to move your opponent around the court: 'You have to understand the strengths and weaknesses of your opponent and make sure that you are not playing into their hands. The most important thing for me was to keep my feet active, make sure that I had my weight moving through the ball at impact to achieve maximum power, and continue to look to move my opponent so I could stay on top of the point. Sometimes it didn't have an immediate effect in a match, but if I was making my opponent run hard I knew there would be a wear-down factor as the match progressed. In that way, more court would eventually open up as your opponent slowed up and that is when your opponent's shot selection may start to fall away.'

Good footwork is an important part of tennis in general but especially for playing for this particular shot: 'Because you are giving up so much open court to the forehand side there is no room for error. You need to get a good read on the ball to make sure you are in the proper position to make a full swing. Giving yourself room to execute the shot is key as the ball is normally tracking into you. Anything less than an aggressive shot will give your opponent a big opportunity to hurt you to the open court.'

Make a promise to yourself that in practice (even in the warm-up) you will make an attempt to hit forehands as much as possible: 'Every ball that lands near the middle of the court must become a forehand and that way your feet will become active from the moment you step on to the court. It will start to feel very natural and become habit in a short space of time. Basket drills are also a valuable learning tool when it comes to practising this shot.'

'Give yourself room to execute the shot.'
STEFFI GRAF

Carlos Moya, a former world No. 1 and French Open champion, on 'HOW TO HIT AN INSIDE-OUT FOREHAND' ...

This must never be a defensive shot: 'When you play an inside-out forehand, you're too far from the middle of the court, and you've left a lot of open court on the forehand side. You have to make sure you hit a good shot, as otherwise you're going to lose the point.'

Eighty per cent of the time, you have a feeling before your opponent hits the ball that you're going to run around your backhand to play an inside-out forehand: 'This is sometimes difficult to see from the outside, but once you're inside the court and you're playing, you get a feel for when you're going to have time to play this shot.'

Balance is important, as you're moving quickly to get into position, then you stop and wait there for a fraction of a second before hitting the ball: 'It's very easy to lean too far to the left. Then you lose direction, you lose control and you lose power.'

Get used to hitting the ball a little closer to your body than you would with a regular forehand: 'This is because you don't have time to move so far around to give yourself more space.'

Most of the time you hit the shot with an open stance: 'You can also hit it semi-open, it doesn't really matter. But never closed.'

Laura Robson, a former junior Wimbledon champion, on 'HOW TO ATTACK WITH YOUR FOREHAND' ...

The biggest mistake you can make when attacking with your forehand is trying to smash every ball, as a lot of them will end up in the back fence:

'Give yourself some margin. Don't just think that it's all about hitting the ball hard, because it isn't.'

You have to create the right opportunities to play an attacking forehand: 'You need to work the point, and to create the chances to attack. So you need to work on all parts of your game, and use all of your game, so that you can attack with your forehand.'

Roger Federer and Pete Sampras' former coach Paul Annacone on 'THE IMPORTANCE OF YOUR COURT POSITION WHEN PLAYING A FOREHAND' ...

No matter what level you are playing at, the middle area of the court is key: 'If you control the middle area of the court, you will get neutral balls and can then be offensive with your forehand, to either side of the court. A key component, not discussed enough, is that if you are in the middle of the court dictating, you already have great court position, so you can adjust easily from there to cover a lot of ground. After using your forehand, you will be looking for the finishing ball, either the very short forehand or the easy volley to knock off the winner.'

Fernando Verdasco, a former Australian Open semi-finalist, on 'HAVING REALISTIC EXPECTATIONS FOR YOUR FOREHAND' ...

You have to get the balance right between going for your shots and taking too many risks: 'Play on the practice court as you plan to on the match court.'

Hitting some big forehands early on will give you confidence for the rest of the match: 'That leaves me feeling good about myself and my game.'

When you miss an easy forehand on an important point, that's going to hurt you more than in a regular point. But appreciate that you will make mistakes – no one can play a perfect match: 'You have to hit so many balls during a match, it's just not possible to do everything perfectly.'

Angelique Kerber, who reached her first grand slam semi-final at the 2011 US Open, on **'HOW TO HIT A FOREHAND DOWN THE LINE'** ...

Play the shot with a little more topspin than you would do if you were going cross-court: 'It's a more difficult shot than going cross-court because when you go down the line you are trying to hit the ball over the highest point of the net. The extra topspin will help lift the ball over the net. But you just need a little bit more, not too much, as a flatter shot will be more aggressive.'

You can't play down the line when you are behind the baseline: 'If you're a long way back, it's better to go for cross-court. Get back into the rally and then, if you have a shorter ball, and you're moving forward, go for that forehand down the line.'

Jelena Jankovic, a former world No. 1, on **'HOW TO HIT THE BALL DOWN THE LINE'** ...

Have forward momentum as you strike the ball: 'Of course, sometimes your opponent hits the ball hard and deep, and you're falling backwards when you hit your shot, but if it's at all possible you want to be moving forward.'

You're hitting the ball over the highest point of the net – but embrace the risk: 'Most players don't feel that comfortable playing this shot as there isn't much margin. For most people, hitting down the line is just not a percentage shot, so they just want to hit cross-court most of the time. But the more you play the ball down the line, the more comfortable you're going to be doing it. With many players, you know that they are going to play a few shots cross-court and then, when they think the opportunity is there, they will go for the forehand or backhand down the line. I like to be ready to go down the line before my opponent is.'

You have to adjust from surface to surface: 'If you're playing on clay, you maybe add some more spin and more height as the points are longer and you have to be patient and construct the point a bit more. But, on grass, the points are much shorter, and so you have to be more aggressive.'

Tracy Austin, twice a US Open champion,
on 'HOW TO HIT THE PERFECT GROUNDSTROKE' ...

Footwork is half the battle: 'You need to make sure you're balanced. And you don't want to get too close to the ball.'

Preparation: 'An early take-back is crucial so you're ready. You need a good shoulder turn. Most people think open stance means everything open. Lower body open but the upper body (shoulders and hips) still needs to turn for you to get power. A good indicator is if you have your name on your back, then with any groundstroke, your opponent should be able to see a few of the letters.'

Load up and hit smoothly: 'The power will come from your legs. Like any shot, it works when your body has everything working together, in unison. So you load from your legs, hit a nice fluid swing, a relaxed swing, and build up racket-head speed. A lot of people try to hit the ball hard but then their muscles tighten up – that's not the right way. Build up the racket-head speed and then square the racket head at impact, that's crucial.'

Andy Murray, who in 2013 became the first British man to win Wimbledon for 77 years,
on 'HOW TO HIT A DROP SHOT' ...

Disguise is the most important part of this shot: 'If your opponent sees it, he's going to get there. For me, it's a lot easier for players with double-handed groundstrokes to disguise that they're about to play a drop shot. Players who use two hands normally take the racket back a little higher, a little bit further up, and then it's a lot easier to just take one hand off, whereas I find it much easier to read opponents who play single-handed groundstrokes.'

Only play a drop shot when you're inside the court: 'You have to be ready to cover the drop shot, if they get it. If you play it at the right time, when you're inside the court, it's a lot easier to cover the angle. If you're too far behind the baseline you can't cover the angles.'

Robin Haase, who has been ranked in the world's top 40,
on 'HOW TO PLAY AN APPROACH SHOT' ...

Don't make the mistake that most people make of thinking you have to hit a winner with an approach shot: 'As the name suggests, this shot is just an approach for something else. The approach shot is the shot you play when you come to net to try to hit a volley winner.'

Attack the ball. Really hit it: 'Most of the time when playing this shot you have to step into the court, rather than playing it behind the baseline.'

Most of the time, hit your approach shot down the line: 'You have to think about where you are on the court, and where your opponent is on the court, as you have to watch out that you're covering the next shot. So the most logical thing to do is to hit your approach shot down the line rather than cross-court as then it's easier to cover.'

Hitting an approach shot short can be a good tactic, especially when you hit it with a lot of slice: 'That will mean that the ball will stay low, especially on a surface like grass. When you hit it short, you have to run into net even more, because the guy can only play cross-court or down the line. You've taken away the lob.'

The biggest mistake you can make is rushing the approach shot, and going into net too quickly: 'You shouldn't already be thinking about the volley or the next step. First hit the ball and then come to the net.'

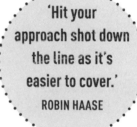

'Hit your approach shot down the line as it's easier to cover.'
ROBIN HAASE

Philipp Kohlschreiber, who has been ranked in the world's top 20,
on 'HOW TO PLAY A SQUASH-SHOT-LIKE RETRIEVAL SHOT' ...

You have to have a very loose wrist. That's because you have to hit the ball with a lot of slice to make sure you are playing a safe shot: 'On the backhand side, you see many guys on the tour slicing when they have to run out wide. It's much tougher on the forehand side. That's because it's much tougher to increase the speed on the ball, and to get the timing right. It's one of the hardest shots to play. You need good touch as you don't have much time to really hit the ball. You're pushing the ball rather than hitting it.'

Most of the time, you should be hitting this shot cross-court rather than down the line: 'Firstly, the court is longer when you go cross-out so you're more likely to keep the ball in the court. Also, the net is a little bit lower when you go cross-court than when you go down the line. So there's a much bigger margin for error. If you're wide of the court, it's better to release the power in a normal way, to go through the ball and have a normal rotation of the body. And that means that you're going to be hitting the ball cross-court. If you want to play down the line, you have to hold the shot for much longer and then there's the possibility that you hit the shot just a split-second too early or too late and then you miss the court. By going cross-court, there's more margin, so if you're a little early or late, you're still going to make your shot.'

You're trying to keep the ball as low as possible: 'It should be as low and as deep as possible in the court, and also be hit at great speed. When you have to run and move before playing the ball, that's the difficult part.'

This shot will vary from surface to surface: 'On clay, the bounce is higher, which makes it much tougher to play the slice. On the other hand, because the surface is slower, it's more likely that you will have time to hit a normal shot. On grass, the ball will be coming to you at a faster speed, so it's a bit easier as then you don't have to generate all the pace yourself.'

Ernests Gulbis, who has been ranked in the world's top 20,
on 'HOW TO HIT THE BALL HARD' ...

Only once you've learned the right technique can you hit the ball hard: 'I see young guys just hitting the ball hard, but without the proper technique – without any balance, or moving the legs. It all starts at a young age. You have to put the right work in. Once you have the right technique and balance, when you grow up and have more power, then you can hit the ball strong. I have naturally clean shots without any robotic movements, and that's why I can hit the ball hard. When it's one fluid movement, you can be strong on your shots. Technique is the most important thing. Many coaches don't understand that. They work on fitness, they work on strength, but I believe that everything starts with technique. And then you build the rest.'

You need muscles (but you need to be patient): 'I hit the ball harder than a lot of players. That's my thing. But I haven't always hit the ball hard. I was growing up at a normal speed – I was small when I was a junior. At 13 or 14, I was the smallest kid, and then at the age of 15 or 16 I started to grow, but I didn't have any muscles. At 17, 18, I started to mature.'

You need a fast wrist and racket-speed: 'You can tell straight away by looking at players whether they can hit the ball strong – or not. Some players have fast racket-speed and acceleration in the wrist.'

Tomas Berdych, a former Wimbledon finalist,
on 'HOW TO HIT YOUR FOREHAND FLAT AND HARD' ...

If you suddenly want to add more power, the biggest mistake you can make is to change your technique: 'If you change your technique, then the shot's gone. You need to always do the same movement on every shot. Every time it should be the same swing. If you try to hit the ball with extra pace, and you're so determined to do it that you get tight, and then you change something in your technique, that's when the ball is going to fly all over the place.'

By standing close to the baseline, or even inside the baseline, you're going to be cutting down on your opponent's time to react: 'You're closer to them, so the ball's going to fly at them.'

How you grip the racket will determine how you hit the ball: 'I hold the racket very straight, and that means it's easier for me to hit the ball flat.'

Daniela Hantuchova, a former world No. 5,
on 'HOW TO GENERATE POWER IN YOUR SHOTS' ...

Stay loose and relaxed, and don't get too stressed or worked up: 'A lot of amateurs make the mistake of really trying to hit it, and they end up forcing the shot, and they will make an error. You need to stay as loose as possible, as that's when you are going to generate the most power, when you're swinging freely, and you're not feeling too tense.'

You need a strong core – that will allow you to keep your body still while hitting the ball: 'You don't want to move your body, as that's when you lose power and control. Get your timing right, and everything will flow from that.'

Eugenie Bouchard, who reached her first grand slam final at Wimbledon in 2014,
on 'HOW TO PLAY A LOB' ...

Don't be scared to hit it: 'It's better to hit it a bit too much and risk the ball being a little bit too high and landing beyond the baseline, rather than under-hitting the shot and giving your opponent a sitter.'

If you're behind the baseline, a lob is more effective than a passing shot because you're further out of position and your opponent is being more aggressive: 'If you hit a passing shot they're more likely to pick it off and to win the point. Of course, you do see crazy passing shots that people hit when they're out wide and on the run, but those aren't easy to play. Those are tough and risky. So, generally the further back you are, the more you should be considering playing a lob.'

When you practise your lob, it's good to do it with someone at the net, so you're actually hitting the shot over someone, and then you can see if they reach the ball or not.

Conchita Martinez, a former Wimbledon champion,
on 'HOW TO PLAY MOONBALLS' ...

Understand that playing a deep, looping shot can drive your opponent crazy: 'You might find yourself playing against an opponent who is very comfortable hitting everything at hip-height. So if you suddenly start putting more height and depth on the shot, and they have to hit the ball from around their shoulder, or even higher, they're going to get frustrated.'

Don't make the mistake of thinking that this is only a defensive shot – it is an aggressive shot, too: 'Hit the ball as deep as you can, and also hit it with as much topspin as possible. To play the shot well, you need some good racket-head speed. Hit the ball hard, and then control it with the spin. You want to drive your opponent as far back as possible, and to have them hitting shots at heights, and in places on the court, that they're not used to.'

The ability to play this shot gives you much-needed variety: 'A lot of players need more options on court, and the ability to play this shot gives them one.'

These shots work better on clay courts and hard courts than on grass: 'Of all the surfaces, clay is probably the best on which to play a high, looping shot as the ball is going to bounce up really high. Plus, if you need it, you're going to have much more time to get back into position – if you have been forced wide, you will want to get back into the centre of the court. You can obviously use this shot on grass, but how effective it is depends on how high the court is bouncing.'

BACKHAND

Stan Wawrinka, who won his first grand slam title at the 2014 Australian Open, on 'HOW TO ATTACK WITH YOUR ONE-HANDED BACKHAND' ...

The legs are very important with this shot – you need to be early with your legs and then you have to commit and go for it: 'With a one-handed backhand, if you're a little bit late, you don't have the left hand [as a right-hander] to help you get the power. You need to be really early with the legs and when you go for it you have to advance through the ball and not wait for it. You have to commit to it and go for it, not just wait and play with it.'

With a one-handed backhand, you should be able to mix it up a bit more than if you have a two-handed backhand: 'You should be attacking with your slice.'

Richard Gasquet, a former Wimbledon and US Open semi-finalist,
on 'HOW TO HIT A ONE-HANDED BACKHAND' ...

Be unpredictable. The main advantage of a one-handed backhand is that players have the ability to mix it up, and to play slice as well as topspin. Using a one-handed backhand makes it harder for your opponent to guess what you're going to do next: 'I am very comfortable at changing spins and directions with my one-handed backhand so it makes it harder for my opponent to guess what shot I will be playing. Sometimes players with a two-handed backhand tend to hit the same way a little too much in cross-court rallies and then attack down the line.'

Stay strong on your front leg: 'You need to load up all your strength on that leg.'

Concentrate on the timing rather than the power of the shot. Move forward towards the ball as you prepare for the shot and hit it early: 'I would say it's difficult for an amateur player to generate as much power with a one-handed backhand as if he or she was using two hands. But you can compensate the loss of power by hitting the ball early. So hit it early and well in front of you.'

Keep your head still throughout the shot and keep your balance while you swing: 'It's essential to avoid the temptation of flipping the top half of your body too soon while looking at the ball leaving the racket. If you do that, it will result in a loss of balance and control of the ball. The best way to master a one-handed backhand is probably to repeat the shot hundreds of times without an opponent on the other side of the court, and not to worry about where the ball goes first but to remain focused on your balance. Your balance is key to hitting a clean shot and making sure the ball remains within the court. Without balance you lose all control over the direction of your shot.'

Your other hand helps you support the shot; by helping you turn your body and offering better control.

David Nalbandian, a former Wimbledon finalist and world No. 3,
on 'HOW TO DEVELOP A WORLD-CLASS TWO-HANDED BACKHAND' ...

A two-handed backhand is good for young players and for amateurs (as well as for professionals) because you feel you have more power and more control over the ball. A good drill for the practice court is to try to hit the ball as soon as it bounces because that will allow you to use your opponent's power as well as your own. 'To turn the shot into more of a weapon, you have to train and train and train – it's the best way to improve it.'

You have to have you feet firmly on the ground if you want to be aggressive with this shot: 'Only then can you prepare the swing and hit the ball properly.'

One hand is for power and the other one for taking aim: 'In my case, I am right-handed, so I use the right hand to give power to my stroke and the left hand to aim at the target and give direction to my stroke.'

You produce most of the power through the legs, but you can generate some extra power through a little turn of the shoulder.

Tim Henman, a former world No. 4, on 'HOW TO HIT A BACKHAND SLICE' ...

A backhand slice will be very effective against an opponent who plays with an extreme grip. Or when you're playing on a surface that keeps low: 'Nowadays, with players using such extreme grips, if you can keep the ball really low, your opponent will struggle to get underneath it.'

> **'This can be an aggressive shot.'**
> TIM HENMAN

You can attack with your slice backhand – it doesn't have to be a defensive shot: 'These days, it is seen as more of a defensive shot because most players are using two-handed backhands, and they don't really have the ability to play a good slice backhand. But, when used well, this can be an aggressive shot.'

When using a backhand slice as an approach shot, you can often take the ball a little earlier.

Don't chop down on the ball too much; you need to make sure you're still going through the ball: 'Make sure your backswing isn't too big. But you need a long follow-through. Make sure you get a good shoulder turn.'

THE VOLLEY AND OVERHEAD SMASH

Martina Navratilova,

a winner of nine Wimbledon singles titles,

on 'HOW TO PLAY A VOLLEY' ...

The biggest misconception that people have about the volley is that you should have a cocked wrist when you hit the ball. Don't do that: 'The wrist needs to be in a neutral position. You should have a firm wrist, but not a cocked wrist, as a cocked wrist limits you. Actually having a cocked wrist causes you to make mistakes – you can't really hit it. If you cock your wrist, the face of the racket actually moves so that it's facing you more, and that means that you will be forced to hit it cross-court. If you want to go down the line, you move your wrist, and that means you lose power. If you keep the wrist flat, you have much more power.'

Keep the elbow close to the rib cage: 'If your arm is a long way from your body, you will lose power, so keep your arm in as much as possible.'

Imagine there's a piece of string from the bottom of your elbow to the ground, holding it in place. There is basically no swing: 'You will swing anyway. But if you think, "I'm not going to swing", you will do a little punch, a little jab.'

Don't try to hit the ball a long way in front of you, as then you'll be stretching and you won't have the power you need: 'You're still hitting the ball in front of you, but not so far out that everything goes wobbly.'

Use your volley to put pressure on your opponent: 'Now everyone hits the ball so well from the baseline, what's going to be the deciding factor? Are you just going to hope that you hit it better than the other guy? Or are you going to get to the net and force your opponent to hit a great shot?'

Rod Laver, who won 11 grand slam singles titles and is considered by some to be 'the greatest', on 'HOW TO IMPROVE YOUR VOLLEY' ...

Hitting a strong volley is a lot like punching someone on the nose: 'You have to put some force into the shot. You're not stroking the ball.'

Don't drop your racket head: 'You always want your racket to be higher than your wrist. That's true even if you are playing a low ball.'

Whenever possible, stand side-on to where you want to hit the ball: 'It's so important to watch the ball as closely as possible. Watch it all the way on to your strings. And, if you have time – you won't always – move your feet so that you're standing sideways on to the net.'

You don't always need a firm wrist: 'It depends what you're trying to do. If you want to punch the ball back deep into the court, then, sure, you need a firm wrist. But if you want to drop the ball short, then you have to relax your wrist and make it a bit more supple. Every shot is different, and you have to be ready to make quick decisions and quick adjustments.'

Jo-Wilfried Tsonga, a former Australian Open finalist, on 'HOW TO HIT A DIVING VOLLEY' ...

Don't think about it too much – just dive: 'If you start thinking how the surface of the court is hard, and how it's going to hurt a lot when you land, you're never going to do it.'

Enjoy the pleasure that comes from hitting this shot: 'When I dive and I win the point, I'm so happy it's like I won the match. And the crowd likes it, too.'

Boris Becker, who won three Wimbledon titles, on 'THE POSSIBLE PITFALLS OF A DIVING VOLLEY' ...

Ideally, you want to avoid playing a diving volley – it's going to hurt: 'You want to be fast enough to get to the ball with your legs. Unfortunately, I sometimes wasn't fast enough, but I didn't want to give up on the ball and the point, so that was why I decided to dive.'

You have to be brave if you want to play this shot – especially if you're going to dive on hard courts, as well as on grass and clay: 'Unfortunately, I

dived on all surfaces – believe me, diving on hard
courts is painful – but I just couldn't stop myself.
It just became something I did, a part
of my game.'

You need to get the technique right with
the roll as otherwise you're going to land on your
wrist or your hip, and you won't be able to walk
any more: 'You won't have much time to think
about it, so a lot of it will come down to instinct. You
should try a few dives in practice before you do them in a
match, and maybe use a soft mat so you don't really hurt
yourself the first few times.'

Jim Courier, a former world No. 1, and a winner of four grand slam titles,
on **'WHEN TO PLAY A SWING OR DRIVE VOLLEY'** ...

With a standard volley, you can only poke at it, but with a swing volley you
should be looking to generate a lot of racket-head speed: 'The reason to play
this shot is that you can play with a lot of power, and really put the ball away.
I've always considered it a fun shot to hit if you like to take some risks. This
was a shot that everyone learned at the Nick Bollettieri Academy and we
were always trying to hit it harder than the next guy.'

Play this like a normal groundstroke – but you have to consider the spin
your opponent has imparted on the ball and what the ball is going to do
when it hits your strings: 'When a topspin shot from your opponent lands
on the court, it loses most of its topspin and it's easy for you to control your
shot. If your opponent is hitting a ball with a lot of heavy topspin, trying to
hit a swinging volley off that is a real challenge.'

Typically, you hit this in mid-court in lieu of a regular approach shot:
'When you play the swing volley you're probably behind the service line,
because if you're inside the service line you can probably just play a higher
percentage volley and poke the ball away. However, some players also opt to
play a swing volley instead of an overhead.'

Leander Paes, a former doubles world No. 1,
on 'HOW TO PLAY A DROP VOLLEY' ...

The power comes from the legs: 'The arms are just for the finesse, and for getting the spin on the ball.'

A lot of people say you should play the drop volley close to the net, and with a very deft touch, but you can also play it with a lot of backspin: 'I use my legs to drive forward and at the same time use my arms to put backspin on the ball. That backspin gives me a little more margin as the ball goes over the net.'

Play this shot with a loose grip, much softer than when you're hitting a firm volley: 'With a firm volley, I hold the racket at about 90 per cent strength – I go boom right through the centre of the ball – but with the drop volley, I use about 30 to 40 per cent strength.'

Disguise is what creates winners with this shot: 'Up to a certain point, I have the same technique playing a drop volley as I do when I'm punching the ball deep. And then I release the grip. The body does almost exactly the same movement – there's maybe a little more drive forward with the legs, and then just before I make contact with the ball, I release the grip a little more.'

The biggest mistake you can make with this shot is hitting it into the net: 'If you've got your opponent out wide and you've got an open court and a fairly comfortable volley, don't try to be too cute with it. You need to give yourself some margin for error. Also, don't play too tight to the net or too close to the lines. And don't get too lazy and try to play the shots with just your arms, that's not going to work. You need to use your legs.'

Dominic Thiem, who was 20 when he broke into the world's top 100,
on 'HOW TO PLAY A HALF-VOLLEY' ...

You shouldn't swing as hard with a half-volley as you would with a regular groundstroke: 'The most important thing is to concentrate on your timing, as you have to time this better than a normal groundstroke. If you're swinging at the ball at full pace, you will make too many mistakes.'

The worst mistake you can make is to lift the ball up too high over the net, as that will give your opponent an easy passing shot: 'You want to keep the ball as low as possible.'

You want to get low to play this shot: 'So bend your knees.'

Don't hold the racket too tightly: 'You need to have good feeling in your hand.'

If you can, don't play a half-volley – move in and play a volley: 'I see the half-volley as an emergency shot. If you have a choice, you should always choose a volley. A half-volley is going to be one of the most difficult shots to play. But of course there are going to be situations when you have to play a half-volley.'

Beware playing a half-volley on clay: 'It's easiest to play this shot on hard courts because there are no bad bounces. It's toughest to play a half-volley on clay, as there are many bad bounces, so you have to time the shot perfectly.'

> **'Keep the ball as low as possible.'**
> DOMINIC THIEM

Max Mirnyi, a former doubles world No. 1, on 'HOW TO HIT SOMEONE AT THE NET' ...

You're trying to win the point whichever way possible – there's nothing wrong with powering the ball down at an opponent: 'Sometimes hitting the ball straight at your opponent is the only option. Your opponent's at the net and there's no time to react. Playing on the professional tour is not like playing at a country club. In men's doubles, hitting an opponent is common practice.'

But don't try to take someone's head off: 'To a certain extent, hitting someone could be seen as a psychological boost. If you try to take someone's head off, and you were directly aiming at the head, and your ball was going out of the back of the court by a mile, that's not going to be taken nicely – it's going to haunt you somewhere down the road. Maybe it will haunt you in that match, or maybe at a later stage. Other players will quickly find about what you did. You will get a bad reputation for doing that, and you will have to watch out.'

If you have your mind set on hitting your opponent to get a psychological edge, then that's fine, but remember there's a risk attached to aiming directly at them: 'If the court is wide open, why take the risk? Your opponent could reflex it back.'

Roberta Vinci, who has held the doubles world No. 1 ranking, on 'HOW TO HIT A SMASH' ...

A smash is well named – you have to hit it: 'You have to have confidence in your shot. Even when it's a sunny day and it's difficult to see the ball, you have to try to play with power, and not just place the ball in the court.'

In both singles and doubles, it's usually better not to hit your smash down the middle, but to go wide to the lines: 'That's especially true when you're playing on grass – if you hit a low, skidding smash that goes wide, that's going to be difficult for someone to get to. However, if you do decide to go through the middle of the court – on grass or any other surface – you need to hit it with a lot of power.'

Don't worry about hitting an opponent with your smash: 'Sometimes, when your opponent is standing really close to the net, you have to hit the ball right at them. You should feel that you can hit the ball wherever you want. If you hit them, just say sorry, and then think about the next point. You have to concentrate on winning the match.'

Footwork is key: 'You have to move your feet to make sure you're in the right place. If you don't move and get into position, you're going to have problems.'

Max Mirnyi on 'HOW TO HIT A BACKHAND SMASH' ...

This is one of the toughest shots in the game, requiring a lot of strength, so you need strong shoulders and back muscles: 'It's tough because you have to generate pace over what is usually a weak part of the body, and it doesn't feel as natural as hitting serves or forehand smashes. You have to generate energy by turning your shoulder and getting your body up and over the ball.'

But try not to over-hit it: 'If you're comfortable with it, put some pace and conviction into the shot. But if you're feeling a bit stuck, and you don't like your position on the court, the first thing you need to think about is getting the ball into play, and whether you can aim for your opponent's backhand side. You can then hopefully recover and get back to where you want to be in the service box. The amount of risk you're willing to take should also depend on what the score is. If you're up by a couple of breaks, why not go for a little more?'

Particularly effective in grass-court doubles, the key to a good backhand smash is timing: 'Good footwork is essential if you're going to get the timing right with this shot. If you can't get a lot of power on the shot, work the angles, or try to hit a ball that keeps low. I don't think players, even professionals, spend enough time practising this shot, but it's part of my routine when getting ready for matches.'

Pat Rafter, a former world No. 1 and US Open champion,
on 'WHY YOU SHOULD PRACTISE YOUR BACKHAND SMASH' ...

Difficult, but surprisingly effective: 'A fun drill on the practice court – I used to do this as a kid – is to try to bounce the ball over the back fence with a backhand smash. It's funny because it's not a shot that people use much. But then when you learn how to play it, you find that you can use it quite a lot. Most people are a bit lazy, and run around and play a normal smash on the other side.'

Pete Sampras, a winner of 14 grand slam singles titles,
on 'HOW TO HIT A SLAM-DUNK SMASH' ...

To play this shot, you have to be athletic and know how to jump, so play some basketball: 'Jumping up for a slam dunk smash isn't that different to jumping up for a basketball shot.'

You can intimidate your opponent with a slam-dunk smash (but make sure you're going to win the point): 'I used to play the shot for a whole bunch of reasons, and one of them was intimidation. It's sending out a message to your opponent that says, "I'm moving well, I'm feeling good, and you're not going to get anything past me today." I also played the shot because it was fun. The crowd used to like it, and get into it, and I enjoyed that. But I only played the shot when I knew that I was going to win the point. The most important thing for me was always winning the point, and I didn't want to risk losing it. There were times when I had to play the shot, but most of the time I had other options.'

Before you can slam-dunk, you need to be able to hit a good overhead and a good serve, and then you have to practise: 'If you're a beginner, don't try this at home. It's not an easy shot to play as it's all about getting the timing of the jump and the swing right. There's a lot that can go wrong. When I was growing up, I messed around with it. I would suggest that you mess around with the shot on the practice court and get comfortable with it before you try it in matches, as you don't want to get it wrong.'

Serve and volley if you want to play this shot more often: 'The more you go into net, the more often you'll have opportunities to slam-dunk.'

> '**If you're a beginner, don't try this at home.**'
> PETE SAMPRAS

OTHER TECHNICAL ASPECTS OF THE GAME

Maria Kirilenko, who has been ranked in the world's top 10, on '**HOW TO IMPROVE YOUR FOOTWORK**' ...

Your first three steps need to be quick, so you can get into position as quickly as possible: 'Some days you go on court and you feel as though your legs are slow and heavy, and you're not moving well. So you have to do some exercises between points – go to the back of the court, and quickly do lots of little steps. Don't do one or two. You have to do about ten. And keep on doing those between points until you feel as though your movement has come back. But once you have got your movement back, you should stop doing the exercises, as you don't want to use up too much energy.'

If you're not balanced, you're going to find it very difficult to hit a good shot. It's essential to understand that lots of mistakes come from poor footwork: 'If you keep on making errors, it could be because your footwork isn't good, and could have nothing to do with the rest of your technique. Everything comes from your feet. If you can get your feet moving quickly, and into the right position, you will find that you can cut a lot of mistakes from your game. So think about your feet and what you do with them – it's such an important part of tennis.'

The hardest surface to get used to again is grass: 'When you play your first match of the season on grass, it feels strange, as you don't feel totally sure about your movement. When I return to the grass, I'm like a ballerina, trying to make delicate movements, and not to slip over. It's different on hard courts, as you go on court and you immediately feel safe. And on clay, you can make sharper movements, and you can slide into your shots. But on grass you need to build up your confidence.'

Garbine Muguruza, who defeated **Serena Williams** in the second round of the 2014 French Open, on **'HOW TO IMPROVE YOUR FOOTWORK'** ...

The best way to understand what you're doing and how you can improve is to film yourself during a practice session or match: 'When I'm training, we tape my practice session as that really helps me.'

Don't waste any energy: 'You want to use minimum effort; if you can get somewhere in two steps and not seven, you should do it in two.'

Be ready to improvise. And react quickly: 'Everything in tennis happens at the last moment. You have to make a quick decision about moving to the ball. You only have a small time to decide. And on the faster surfaces you have even less time to react, so you just need to do everything a bit quicker.'

Eugenie Bouchard, runner-up in the Wimbledon women's singles in 2014, on **'HOW TO MOVE ON GRASS'** ...

The key on grass is to stay low: 'Grass is such a different surface to hard or clay, and I think you need to get low so that you're prepared for your opponent's slices and for the balls that slide and shoot through. The toughest transition in professional tennis is when you go from clay to grass, as they're opposite surfaces, so different, and Roland Garros and Wimbledon are the two slams which are closest together, so that's tough. The glutes and quads are the muscles you need most to stay low, so you'll need to strengthen those and keep them active.'

Wear a pair of shoes with studs or pimples – that should stop you from sliding on the lawn: 'You occasionally see players sliding at Wimbledon, but that's not on purpose, as they could sprain their ankle.'

Don't obsess over a change of surface: 'It's still's tennis; it's still a court. When you play a match, you can't only be thinking about the surface. You need to think about your opponent and the match. You go out and do your thing, play your game, and maybe just make a few adjustments because of the surface.'

Kim Clijsters, a former world No. 1 and grand slam champion, on 'HOW TO SLIDE' ...

Don't do it for show. Only slide if you have to, and there's no other way to reach the ball: 'Sliding takes a big toll on your body; it's far better, if you can, to run fast so that you can reach the ball without having to slide. Having said that, sliding was always part of my personality, as I would do absolutely anything to reach the ball.'

You need to be in excellent shape if you're going to slide – in the off-season, work on your legs, glutes and your core: 'You have to make sure your body is ready to do a slide – after I came back to tennis after having my daughter, I had to wait a while to make sure that everything was ready to go.'

You can slide on all surfaces, not just on soft clay: 'I guess I took that slider with me indoors and also on hard courts. Now when I watch professional tennis, I see more and more players doing it.'

Philipp Kohlschreiber, who appeared in his first grand slam quarter-final at the 2012 Wimbledon Championships, **on 'HOW TO DO THE SPLIT-STEP' ...**

By doing a little jump or split-step, you will be much quicker at reacting to your opponent's shot: 'This is all about getting yourself ready for your next shot. If you're playing well, and pushing your opponent around, you'll know what's coming next. But if you're the guy doing a lot of running, you have to be ready. You should be looking at your opponent and watching his racket and the ball. And then you do the little jump or split-step and then you release the energy to the left or right side. If you stay flat on your feet, you'll be much slower, and there's a chance you'll be on the wrong foot.'

You're moving before the ball comes, but you shouldn't be guessing where your opponent is going to play his shot: 'If you make that small jump, you're already moving before you have to react left or right, and it's much faster that way. What you shouldn't do is guess. So you wait until your opponent has played his shot. But if you time the split-step well, you are set up perfectly to sprint to either side, or to move forward to a drop-shot.'

It's the same principle when you're at net rather than on the baseline: 'It's just that everything goes that much faster, and you have to react even quicker.'

Mansour Bahrami, who is seen as tennis's greatest entertainer, **on 'HOW TO PLAY TRICK SHOTS' ...**

If you want to learn trick shots, it's best to start early. You don't need a coach, you just need to try things: 'I've never had a coach or a tennis lesson in my life. I started doing trick shots with a piece of wood that I found in the street – that was my racket.'

Accept that if you're going to play trick shots you might lose a few more matches, but you'll have the pleasure of making people smile: 'If you do a trick shot and it works it's an unbelievable feeling. But if you lose the point, and even the match, it doesn't matter, as it's just a game. I have lost so many matches in my life because I have always played this way, with trick shots, but I've always loved playing this way as I've made many people smile and that for me is very, very, very important.'

One favourite shot is a drop-shot loaded with so much heavy backspin that it lands on his opponent's side of the net and then bounces back to his side: 'This is a difficult shot. You have to go under the ball as fast as you can and you have to hit the ball so it lands very close to the net on your opponent's side. You can play this shot when you're close to the net and also when you're at the baseline. You just have to have good touch. But be careful – if you don't have a strong wrist you can hurt yourself.'

When the ball goes over your head and you turn your back to the court to play the return through your legs, wait until the ball is just about to bounce for a second time before hitting it: 'If you hit it before, you're going to miss for sure. Three times out of five, I know I'm going to win the point when I play this shot. I will either hit a winner or make the other guy nervous. You have to be very careful with this shot, and I would only recommend it if you have very good coordination with the racket and ball, and have strong wrists, as there's the potential for injuring yourself. But if this shot works, the crowds love it.'

Grigor Dimitrov, who appeared in his first grand slam semi-final at the 2014 Wimbledon Championships, on **'HOW TO PLAY A TWEENER'** ...

You should be looking to hit the ball when it has dropped a little lower and closer to the ground than you would do for a regular shot: 'You have to time the ball almost perfectly in order to have good contact. Wait until the ball is a little lower so then you can rip it with your wrist.'

Everything else, it's all in your imagination, and how much you can improvise: 'You can't really practise a tweener. It comes pretty naturally in the match, in the moment. It's obviously a really tricky shot to play, especially in the tough moments. It's all down to the situation on the court. You never know what's going to happen. Sometimes an opponent catches you off guard, and you have to find a way of getting the ball into play.'

Take pleasure from playing tweeners, especially

if you hit winners with them: 'You can really enjoy these shots. My coach wouldn't necessarily find it more satisfying if I hit a winner with a tweener rather than a regular shot. He would give me so much shit afterwards. And I've noticed that lately I haven't really been into those shots in matches so much, so maybe that's my game changing a little bit, and because I'm starting to understand there are more important things than hitting shots like these. I hate myself for that, ha ha.'

Roger Dalton, the head stringer at the Wimbledon Championships,
on **'HOW TO SELECT THE RIGHT STRINGS AND TENSION'** ...

Juniors and club players should go for the softest strings they can. Especially juniors, as the stiffer strings can damage their muscles and joints as they grow: 'Amateurs should be looking at using soft strings that will last them the longest period of time. There's no point using strings that are going to break within an hour. Those stiff strings, used by the professionals, are good for spin and durability and control, but not necessarily the best thing for vibration and shock and jarring of the joints. Once you're physically strong and mature, the stiff strings are fine.'

Lower tension strings give longevity: 'Juniors should be using the lowest tension they can, as that will prevent fatigue. With a lower tension, and a softer string, you're going to have a much longer career. You will also have greater depth on your shot. Older players tend to like a lower tension too, as it gives them easy power.'

However, don't drop your tension so slow that you're always hitting the back fence: 'If you feel as though you're losing control over your shots, you need to play with a higher tension.'

Work out whether you prefer just polyester, just natural gut, or a combination of the two: 'It's about finding the right combination of strings that will give you the right spin, control, comfort and power. Roger Federer, for example, uses a combination of different strings – natural gut in the main strings and a polyester-type string in the cross. Natural gut, made from beef intestine, is still used by a lot of professional players. But they find it a little bit too powerful, so they are dampening down that power with a stiffer, less resilient polyester string. Andy Murray uses polyester in the main string and natural gut in the cross – so the opposite way to Federer. Murray goes for that combination as he found natural gut in the main strings a little bit too powerful. So Murray is dampening down the power, and giving himself some control and spin, by using polyester in the main strings. The main strings are usually the main driver of spin and control, and the cross strings give comfort and power. Some players do have only polyester. But that doesn't give you much feel and power. It will give you oodles of control, but you're losing out on power.'

While it's cheaper using polyester strings, as they don't break so quickly and last longer, that could be a false economy: 'I'm always telling parents that they could end up spending more on physiotherapist's bills than they would have done on more expensive strings.'

Think about the conditions every day: 'On a warm day, the balls are going to fly faster through the air, so you want to increase the tension. And go for a lower tension on a cold or windy day. You have to take altitude, surface and balls into consideration when choosing a tension. The balls are different from tournament to tournament. You might want to bring the tension down if you need more depth on your shots. Of course, it's not going to be possible to make changes if you have already started a match, unless you do what some of the professionals do and have several rackets strung at different tensions.'

> **'On a warm day, the balls are going to fly faster.'**
> ROGER DALTON

Roger Dalton
on 'HOW TO LOOK AFTER YOUR RACKET' ...

Be extremely demanding: 'Professional tennis players are very particular about their rackets, and so they should be. I don't ever mind a player who says they want things done this way or that way. Some players, such as the Williams sisters, ask for their grips to be covered with plastic, as they don't want anyone else touching them. Players competing at Wimbledon can be very particular about the exact time of day they want a racket strung. That's because, with the strings losing tension all the time, they know that the racket will be just right for them when they go on court. It's important to be demanding, as that makes a difference to your game. Some professional players will often send some rackets back to be restrung during a match, as they're not entirely happy.'

Make sure that the grip is the same size on every racket – you want consistency in everything. If possible, always get your rackets strung by the same stringer: 'The top players employ a stringing company that travels with them to all the tournaments, so their rackets will be strung by the same guy on the same machine in the same way and at the same time of day. It's about consistency. You don't want to be worrying about your racket. You want to pick it up and know that you've got the tension you asked for.'

If you're serious about your game, the absolute minimum is to get a freshly strung racket for every match: 'And maybe have some other rackets that have been slightly used as a back-up. Obviously you have to think about costs. Ideally, you would want to go on court with six freshly-strung rackets, but that's going to cost a lot of money.'

Practise with a racket that is strung at the same tension as the one you will use in the match: 'If you've grooved your shots on the practice court, and then in the match you use a racket with a very different tension, that's going to make a big difference. That could change the depth of your shots by three or four inches. That's why you see pros changing their rackets every ball change. Roger Federer changes his racket based on whether he's serving or receiving. If he's serving he will keep the racket for an extra game, as the racket has lost a bit of tension, which gives him some more oomph. However, if he's receiving he will change the racket.'

Most decent juniors will have between four and six rackets. More senior players will have eight rackets: 'One racket is not enough.'

Club players should change their strings as many times a year as they play per week: 'So if you play twice a week, change your strings twice a year. That will keep your strings at a reasonable tension, and nice and resilient and fresh. If you can afford to do that more often, you will have a more consistent game.'

The worst thing you can do is to leave your rackets in the car on a hot day. Or leave them anywhere that's freezing cold: 'You want to avoid exposing your rackets to extremes of temperature.'

When travelling to a tournament, it's a good idea to take a couple of decently strung rackets with you: 'That's a good insurance policy, as you don't know whether the stringing service will be any good when you get there. If you turn up and the stringer is absolutely awful, you are not going to have any rackets to play with.'

When flying abroad with your rackets, wrap them in towels before checking them in with your luggage: 'Putting rackets in the hold of a plane can mess them up.'

Gordon Reid, one of the world's leading wheelchair tennis players,
on **'HOW TO GET STARTED IN WHEELCHAIR TENNIS'** ...

Just go for it and give it a try. And have fun: 'It's a really fun sport that can be played by anyone. It's fast-paced and skilful, that's why I enjoy it. I know from my own experience you get so much more out of the game if you're enjoying yourself. Find a friend or family member to share the journey with.'

To begin with you can use an everyday chair, to learn the shots and technique. But to really make the most of the sport you need a sports chair: 'There are many clubs that now keep a stock of sports wheelchairs to be used by new players.'

As it can be a bit frustrating at first when the movement in the chair is new, start off using a smaller court and maybe using softer balls while you're still learning the movement: 'The hardest part of the game is being in the right position every time to be able to hit an aggressive shot. This takes time to master. I would recommend doing a lot of movement drills that involve sharp turning and short-distance sprints. Also, as it is a tough sport on the upper body, injury prevention and flexibility are both an integral part of top players' training.'

The biggest mistake you can make is to get into the habit of pushing the chair without holding your racket in your hand: 'Whenever you are on court always try to push with your racket against the wheel and avoid putting it on your lap or between your legs.'

Esther Vergeer, the most successful wheelchair player in history,
who was undefeated for a decade,
on **'HOW TO IMPROVE YOUR WHEELCHAIR TENNIS'** ...

Women should train with the men: 'I used to train with men all the time. They're faster, they're stronger, they're quicker, and it raised my level a lot.'

Get mentally stronger – that means staying calm on court and making the right decisions: 'The other girls were so close to beating me – they had the skills and physically they could have done it – but sometimes they weren't mentally stable enough to make it work.'

Find a coach who helps to give you that calm: 'Working with a coach who comes from able-bodied tennis, he had a lot of experience and taught me amazing stuff, not only on the court but also off it – like how your attitude should be and how you should approach matches, training, other people, the media. My confidence was so high, on and off the court, and that gave me a lot of calm.'

Work harder on every aspect of the game: 'I did a lot of mobility training in my chair; I did a lot of fitness training for my upper body so I think I was maybe a little stronger than the average girl.'

THE MENTAL GAME

BEING A WINNER

Maria Sharapova, who won Wimbledon at 17, and who has won all four grand slam titles, **on 'HOW TO BE MENTALLY TOUGH' ...**

Take responsibility for yourself – you have to be mature enough to realise that the most important thing is what you do, not what anybody else does: 'I think it's something that's within. Of course, everyone is going to have difficult moments, but it's really about how you get up from those moments. You can have the best people in the world helping you, but if you don't tell yourself to grow up inside, and to be positive and strong, then you won't ever become mentally tough.'

Don't obsess over the past, and don't imagine that the same approach will work twice – look to the future and be flexible: 'Every single moment in everybody's life is different and I've never been one to look back at something and think, "That worked for me that time and it will work for me again this time."'

Alize Cornet, a former junior champion at Roland Garros,
on 'HOW TO PLAY WELL IN FRONT OF A HOME CROWD' ...

Do what you can to get the crowd in your pocket: 'Sometimes a crowd can be tough on home players – that happens at Roland Garros and I don't always understand why. If they're against you, that can be terrible. So it's important to have the crowd on your side, as they can be so powerful. When you play a good shot, and you have the crowd yelling and screaming and going crazy, that's such a great feeling. To get the crowd on your side, you must share some of your positive emotions with them. If you have a good moment, show the crowd what it means to you. That helps them get into the match, and start supporting you. You also have to fight like a lion. The crowd wants to see that you're giving your all. If they think you're not trying your best, they are not going to like it.'

There's going to be extra pressure playing in front of a home crowd – so try not to think too much about who is watching you: 'On the one hand, it's great playing at home as you get the support from all your friends and family who have come to see you play. But then there's the extra pressure, as you want to play well for the people who have come to see you. But you must block that out. Don't start looking for people in the crowd either. The emotional side of playing at home can be the toughest part – that can really burn you out. One way of dealing with that is to think that, for the rest of the year, you manage on your own without a home crowd.'

Don't be too sociable when you're at your home tournament – if you spend too much time talking to people at the tournament site, you won't have any energy left for your matches: 'For example, at Roland Garros, I could spend all day talking to people I know and like, but that uses up so much energy. It's best for me to be back relaxing at the hotel.'

Roger Rasheed, who has coached Grigor Dimitrov, Gael Monfils, Jo-Wilfried Tsonga and Lleyton Hewitt, on 'THE IMPORTANCE OF HAVING A STRONG WORK ETHIC' ...

Exhaust your day: 'Your work ethic is one thing that you can control. My advice to club players and juniors is to be positive each day as the game challenges you. My approach to coaching is all about exhausting your day in a positive way, which will give you the best chance to develop and chase your dream. A strong work ethic is important in life – only if you have one can you expect positive outcomes.'

Think long term and keep the faith: 'To become an elite or great player takes time, and you have to be prepared to put in that time, while at the same time being in a hurry. You need to have a plan and to see the bigger picture, and [you shouldn't] doubt yourself.'

Don't think working hard means you have to spend hours and hours on the practice court: 'Train hard, but smart. It's not always about how much time you have spent on court.'

Work hard at improving the strongest parts of your game: 'Make your strengths as strong as possible as that will determine the outcome of your matches.'

Rafa Nadal's coach and uncle, Toni, on 'HOW TO HAVE A STRONG WORK ETHIC' ... (Rafa Nadal has achieved the career golden slam, winning all four grand slam titles as well as the Olympics.)

Don't expect instant results. You have to be prepared to work for a long time: 'The problem in this life is that young people want everything quickly and they don't always want to work, work, work. But you do need to work. Maybe someone needs just one hour to learn how to do something – like how to play a topspin forehand – and someone else needs two hours, but *you* need ten hours, or even twenty. You need to be mentally prepared that it could take a long time.'

If you work well and work hard, you can do anything: 'Nothing in this life is that difficult.'

Li Na, a multiple grand slam champion,
on 'HOW TO DEAL WITH EXPECTATION' ...

Try not to care about what people say about you: 'In the beginning, I could not forget what people said. I was taking all the bad things personally. I was thinking: "I'm bad, I was lucky to win a grand slam." But afterwards, I was like: "OK, so I am lucky. It doesn't matter. I have a grand slam in my pocket, doesn't matter how."'

Remember that it's better to be talked about than not: 'It's not easy to cope with all the attention. At the beginning, after winning my first grand slam at the 2011 French Open, I was feeling terrible, really, because my life had changed totally. I was a little bit shy so I just didn't want to show up and play matches and see people. But I realised that people will always say something about you, so you can't worry about what they say. Think of it as, "at least people are paying attention to what I'm doing." You have to see the positive side to it.'

Roy Emerson, a winner of 12 grand slam singles titles,
on 'HOW TO BE HUMBLE' ...

You shouldn't have a big celebration on the court after winning a match: 'There's plenty of time and opportunity for that off the court. So wait until you get off the court. When you're on the court, show some respect to your opponent by keeping control of yourself. I know that anyone who wins a grand slam tends to climb up into the stands, and that TV loves that, but I don't think it's right.'

Don't get carried away: 'After all, it's only a tennis match. Think about how you're conducting yourself.'

During the match, don't celebrate too much if you've just hit a good shot: 'That's not very sporting, is it?'

Boris Becker, who first won Wimbledon at the age of 17,
on 'HOW TO HAVE PRESENCE ON COURT' ...

Don't be afraid of a challenge – if you're naturally aggressive and competitive, then it's OK to be like that on court: 'Tennis is a one-on-one sport – it's one man against one man, or one woman against one woman, and my strategy was known. I always wanted to win and I'm a big guy. I never minded a confrontation. And that's how it came across. I was just naturally very aggressive.'

Don't back off if your opponent starts trash-talking you – they have to know that you mean business: 'I would never back off. If I hadn't said something back, maybe that would have harmed my game in some way. You're talking about competing against players like John McEnroe and Jimmy Connors and Ivan Lendl. It was normal – we all did it. If you're an amateur playing at your local club, and you opponent says something, should you respond? That depends on your personality. Not everybody should do that.'

But don't try to fake it, as people will see through you: 'Tennis players are always sending messages to each other with their body language. But it has to be instinctive. Your behaviour has to fit your personality. Not everyone's as aggressive as I was, and that's fine. You can't be someone that you're not.'

You can have a presence or an aura by winning a lot of matches and titles: 'Look at Roger Federer, he's not an aggressive guy. But he's won all those grand slams, and has an aura about him.'

> **'Your behaviour has to fit your personality.'**
> **BORIS BECKER**

Rod Laver, the only man to twice win all four grand slams in one season, on 'HOW TO THINK LIKE A CHAMPION' ...

Believe in your game. Play some shots. And, whatever you do, don't panic: 'Are you going to play steady all your life, or are you going to play some shots? Some days it will work for you, some days it won't. If you want to be a success, you have to feel that you're playing the right game, and really believe in yourself. So much of this is about confidence – when I look back at my career, so much came from being assured of my game and that I was playing the right way.'

Don't expect to play the perfect match: 'That's never going to happen, so you will get frustrated. Winning matches isn't about playing perfectly.'

Be lucky: 'Being a champion is sometimes about having good fortune. Some players produce great tennis but never get the breaks.'

Don't quit. Learn from your defeats: 'Too many players get so upset after losing matches they start thinking "I can't play this game", and they think about quitting. But I always tried to learn from defeats. Remember when you were a child. You were happy after a win, and you were a little sad after losing, but not too sad. Don't linger over your defeats.'

Enjoy yourself: 'As a kid you play the game because you enjoy it. You have that love for the game. You don't want to lose that. You have to work hard to become a champion – there's no magic secret – but you have to enjoy yourself.'

Mats Wilander, a former world No. 1,
on 'HOW TO HAVE STRONG BODY LANGUAGE ON COURT' …

Make sure your opponent can't miss your fist pump: 'Roger Federer always seems to do his fist pumps when he has his back turned to his opponent, what is the point of that? You're trying to fire yourself up, and to show your opponent that you mean business and that you're for real, so doing a fist pump when you're facing the other way, that's just pointless. You can't be so proud that you assume your game is always going to be good enough to win matches; sometimes, you need to be in an opponent's head, even a little bit. So, please, don't copy Roger here. Try to be a bit more like Lleyton Hewitt, and fill your matches with fist pumps.'

Never give your opponent anything: 'If you miss a shot, and think that you should have taken a different option – perhaps you went for the passing shot, and now think a lob would have been better – don't let your opponent know. Don't say anything, and don't go through the motions of playing the shot that you should have played.'

Anger is OK, but disappointment isn't: 'Anger lets your opponent know that you care. But you have to snap out of it fast. Just look at John McEnroe – he goes crazy, and then he forgets about it. But disappointment, with the sloping shoulders and the dropped head, that's not good. That tells your opponent that you are having negative thoughts, that you're living in the past and that you're going to be playing some shitty tennis. Anything like that encourages your opponent.

> 'Fill your matches with fist pumps.'
> **MATS WILANDER**

Body language is important, because it sends messages to your opponent. Would players like Marat Safin and Andy Murray have been better players if their body language was better? Maybe not. But you can be sure that their opponents would have played worse tennis, because they would have looked down the court and seen that the guy was up for it. You don't want to give your opponent anything for free. Show them that you're out there to fight.'

Annabel Croft, a former British No. 1, on 'HOW TO IMPROVE YOUR BODY LANGUAGE' ...

You're going to need a good walk: 'You can learn from Serena Williams, who has an air of confidence. Or look at how Maria Sharapova struts around. Remember how Steffi Graf used to walk around as though she was carrying a briefcase? All those women mean business. They have a purpose about them. As you walk around, you want to project your inner confidence.'

Don't have droopy shoulders or let your head drop. If you can, watch videos of yourself. You will be surprised: 'I'm sure if I had watched tapes of myself back, I would have been horrified by my body language. Most players probably don't realise the messages that they are giving out. So watching clips of yourself is the best way to improve. Body language is massive in tennis. You're giving off so many messages. As an player's, you're always reading a player's body language to see where they're at emotionally. You want to look down the other end of the court, and think, "Ooh, I'm getting to them." Big swings of momentum can come about because you're reading an opponent's body language, or because they are reading yours.'

Ilie Nastase, a former world No. 1, on 'HOW TO INTIMIDATE YOUR OPPONENT' ...

Pick your opponents wisely: 'All the guys who complained against me, the ones I beat through intimidation, were lousy players. Bjorn Borg never complained like that, he just beat me. Stan Smith was the same. Once you complain that somebody bothers you, it's all over inside.'

You can't win just through intimidation. That's impossible. Only do it if you can back it up on court: 'You have to have talent. And you have to be very strong mentally because you have to be able to play the points as well. You cannot just look at an opponent and stop him, for example. That was working maybe 30 years ago when I was playing, but now it doesn't work like that. You have to be good enough to win with your tennis as well.'

Leander Paes, a former doubles world No. 1, on 'HOW TO INTIMIDATE WITH YOUR AURA' ...

Put your opponents under constant pressure: 'You can do that if, like me, you have a big aura. I'm 5ft 10in, and a lot of my opponents are 6ft or taller, but one of the reasons that the guys think I'm an intimidating player is that I have a big aura. I read the game so well, so I'm always creating pressure for my opponents. All the great players have an aura, even in the locker-room, not just on the court.'

Winning is the ultimate way to build an aura, but you can also do so by being very professional at all times, and having a clean and healthy lifestyle: 'You want your colleagues to see you putting the time in. You want them to see you going for a run in the morning; you want them to see you spending more time in the gym. You want them to see that you don't drink or smoke or have late nights. You want them to see that you're always in good shape, that you're looking fresh, that you're happy, you're positive, you're living a lifestyle that is very clean and professional. As much as I love tennis, and I'm passionate about tennis, it is my job. So when I go to the tournament site, I'm on work time. I don't want to just hang about. After a match you ice yourself, you get your stretching done, you do all the right things, but you don't just hang about. I do all these things because they genuinely work for me. But at the same time my rivals will see me doing them and will think, "Whoa, we need to be ready."'

You know that your opponents are intimidated when they start playing risky shots and making lots of unforced errors: 'Tennis is a very instinctive sport. Competition creates a raw animal instinct. Everyone is watching the big players to see what they're doing and how they are looking. An aura builds up, and it causes opponents to go for more and more risky shots, and they're not going to keep on hitting winners – they'll be making a lot of unforced errors.'

Radek Stepanek, who has been ranked in the world's top 10, on 'HOW TO UNDERSTAND GAMESMANSHIP' ...

When your opponent is playing incredible tennis, when he gets hot and is hitting winners from everywhere, you try to slow him down and to break his rhythm: 'For example, some players go to the bathroom after a set, and some players call the physio or trainer on court because he needs to be re-taped or he has an injury. There are things that can be done to distract a guy who is in great rhythm and in the zone. Nobody will tell you that they didn't actually need to go to the bathroom, or that they didn't have an injury, and it's impossible for other people to investigate that. But I can say that I've never left the court for the bathroom if I didn't need to go, and I've never called a physiotherapist on court if I didn't have a real injury problem. But each person knows themselves what they are doing.'

Some players slow their opponents down by walking around at the back of the court between points, and by towelling themselves down: 'I wouldn't recommend that juniors use any of these tactics. I don't think it's the right way.'

Mats Wilander, a winner of seven grand slam singles titles, on 'HOW TO GET INTO AN OPPONENT'S HEAD' ...

Don't start trash-talking or saying abusive stuff over the net. You don't want your opponent to hate you, as he will probably play better tennis: 'In the 1970s players said abusive stuff over the net, but not so much any more. You don't do that. You try to create a reason for somehow hating your opponent. That could be his personality or his game. You try to find something. You try to find something else to fight against. At the same time, you don't want the other guy to hate you. So you have to be the nice guy in one way, as you don't want to piss them off. I believe that 90 per cent of the professionals are better players when their opponent has pissed them off. So I think most of the time you should try to be a really nice guy and then when you have a chance, you give them the fist pump in their face.'

Another good way of psyching out your opponent is to go straight for their strength: 'I used to serve and volley to Ivan Lendl's forehand on the first point, and he would be thinking, "What's wrong with you?" And then you do it again and again.'

Jo-Wilfried Tsonga, a former Australian Open finalist, on 'HOW TO ENJOY YOURSELF ON COURT' ...

Don't treat tennis like it's something real: 'No matter what the sport gives you, it's a game. You need to take pleasure out of being on court because otherwise you need to do something else. Life is all about simple pleasures. I think some people forget that it's a game. People treat sport like it's something real, but we're all actors. I'm maybe not the same on court as I am outside the court.'

Get the crowd involved in your match – they want to be entertained: 'I've always liked to involve the crowd. I like to take care of the people around me. They have come to see you for a reason, and that's to be entertained. I'm on the court to take pleasure, and also to entertain the people around me. I can't behave as if they're not there. I'm not going to ignore them. For me, that's not possible.'

Li Na, who at the 2011 French Open became the first Chinese woman to win a grand slam singles title, on 'HOW TO BE HAPPY AS A TENNIS PLAYER' ...

You might not be able to change the world but you can change yourself – before trying to make others happy, make sure that you're happy: 'I like to have a happy team, but the most important thing, as a tennis player, is for me to be happy. Before, I was a negative person, and I always felt everything was bad. I changed that. So you can change. If you're sad, you have to keep going. You can change. I changed. And now because I'm happy, everyone around me is happy.'

Your mood off the court will affect how you feel on it, so try to think positively before you walk out to compete: 'If I am feeling sad or bad when I start a match, I always play badly. I start thinking the bounce is no good; the weather is bad. If you are happy, you play well.'

Henri Leconte, a former French Open finalist,
on 'HOW TO TAKE PLEASURE FROM YOUR TENNIS' ...

Don't become obsessed: 'You play to have a good time. At my club, there are people who are so focused on winning – they're crazy about doing everything they can to win matches – that they don't have any time to have fun. And if you're not having fun, you should be doing something else with your time.'

Be yourself – don't try to be someone you're not: 'I have my own personality; my character and I play with the crowd. I'm different to lots of other players. Does expressing your emotions make you play better tennis? That depends on your character. Everything depends on your character. Some people are more introverted than me, and that's their character. You can't change your personality. John McEnroe went nuts on the court, he went crazy, but that's just how he is.'

Ivan Lendl and Andy Murray's former psychologist Alexis Castorri, on 'HOW TO PLAY YOUR BEST TENNIS' ...

Every athlete should have a repeatable 'routine' or 'system' that they use before competing: 'The mind and body work together, so devising a system that progressively relaxes and then sharpens the focus in preparation for competing is essential. For example, dynamic stretches, followed by cardio, followed by deep stretching, followed by visualisation of performance. For each person this is different, the point being to develop a system that works for you and then stick to it.'

Developing awareness of who you are, your personality strengths and the areas needing improvement, is the first step towards identifying goals: 'I am a psychologist and a therapist as well as a sports psychologist. Therefore my interest is first and foremost the person. I prefer to "use" an innate strength a person already has within them to assist in attaining their life and sports goals. Your entire life should be a reflection of who you are, what's important to you, and what you bring to the table that we can tap into to attain success.'

Relax the body and remove any tension before the match: 'I've been in practice over 25 years. Back in the early days with my tennis clients, no one was doing any form of stretching outside of a few quick movements with their rackets. For me, it just made sense that to relax the body and remove any tension was important for both mental and emotional preparation, so I recommended yoga, which no one was doing at the time. I still believe in this concept and therefore recommend a good 20–25 minutes of stretching before playing.'

An essential truth to performing well is that you won't play at your best when you are focused on outcomes: 'Focus instead on the specific task at hand; for example, coming in on the right ball or staying low through impact. When your mind starts tracking and wanting to know how the match is going to turn out, you have stopped playing the match. You have stopped competing, you have stopped doing everything you can to perform at your best.'

The pre-match goal is not having a clear mind, but a mind filled with the right thoughts: 'For each player, these thoughts may be a bit different, but generally they should include a strong focus on what they want to accomplish out there today, some sense of their game plan, a feeling of commitment to keep the mind on one thing at a time in the most positive way possible and making sure they use the time between points to motivate and inspire themselves.'

Jamie Murray, Andy's older brother, on 'SIBLING RIVALRY' ...

(Jamie was the first of the Murray brothers to win a Wimbledon title, with success in the mixed doubles competition in 2007 when he partnered Jelena Jankovic.)

It's OK to wind your brother or sister up: 'That's normal, especially with two brothers. All brothers fight. But there is a limit. I once hammered Andy's hand. I think we were nine or ten, and he had beaten me in the final of a tournament, and we were coming back home, and he was winding me up about the match. He had his hand on his knee. I turned around and hammered it with my fist. His nail was broken and it took about 15 years to fully recover. Even now it's still a bit messed up.'

Appreciate it's not going to be easy playing against your sibling in a tournament – unless you really don't like them: 'It's a totally different feeling when you compete in a tournament against your sibling. Part of you doesn't want to see your brother lose. You know what to expect, as you know each other's game really well. But I guess it's more of a mental thing than anything else. You're looking down the court at your brother and that's who you're trying to beat. It's a weird feeling, it's not a natural thing to want to see your brother lose.'

You're always going to have someone to play with and someone to spur you on. Embrace it: 'Andy and I are very similar in age – there are only 15 months between us – and when we were growing up I was always a little bit better than him. It was probably better for him having an older brother. He was always trying to beat me and I'm sure that spurred him on. That helped his development somewhat. We were always pushing each other.'

Urszula Radwanska, a former junior Wimbledon champion, whose older sister Agnieszka won the junior title and has played in a senior final,
on 'HOW TO MAKE THE MOST OF SIBLING RIVALRY' ...

Embrace the friendship: 'Tennis is very much an individual sport, so it's important to realise how lucky you really are in having your best friend around. Aga and I share a room whenever we play the same tournaments and it's always a lot of fun.'

Don't take yourself too seriously: 'The key to our success is that once we're done with tennis for the day, we can relax in each other's company and not think about forehands and backhands.'

Stan Wawrinka, an old friend of **Roger Federer** who won his first grand slam title at
the 2014 Australian Open, **on** 'HOW TO LEARN FROM A FRIEND'S SUCCESS' ...

Take note of everything your friend is doing to prepare for matches – you
can take little things from people: 'When I joined the tour Roger Federer was
already there, he was the best, and we had a good relationship, so I took the
chance to practise with him. I also took the chance to look at what he was
doing, how he was practising, how he was playing, and also to talk with him
and to learn. I'm not saying you have to do the same thing – but I think it's
always interesting to see what others are doing.'

Be a good listener: 'Roger always gave me advice about whoever I was
playing.'

Chris Evert, a former world No. 1,
on 'HOW TO PLAY AGAINST A FRIEND, A SIBLING OR
SOMEONE YOU CARE ABOUT' ...

Avoid eye contact: 'I hated playing against someone I cared about, whether
that was a close friend or my sister. Playing my sister made me feel sick to
my stomach. It was the worst, absolutely horrible. I didn't want to lose. I
didn't want them to lose either. My way of dealing with playing someone
I was emotionally connected with was to avoid looking into their eyes. I
didn't want any emotion out there. I played my best tennis when I avoided
all emotion and drama. Emotion would get in the way of my job as a
professional tennis player, which was to win matches. If you look into their
eyes, you will see how much they want to win, and you will see, if you're
winning, how disappointed they are. That's not great to look at. If you can't
see their eyes, it's much easier not to be emotionally involved.'

Summon up the killer instinct – you're on court to win a tennis match
so don't feel sorry for your opponent: 'I was known for my killer instinct.
When I was playing someone I didn't know or care about, that came easily
to me, as I didn't feel anything. But when the girl at the other side of the net
was a friend or my sister, I had to work three times as hard to have that killer
instinct. Because you have to have that killer instinct.'

It's OK to talk to your friend or sibling before you go on court: 'You
should be able to say, "Good luck."'

Play the ball, and not the opponent: 'You have to try to ignore who you're playing against, treat this as any other match.'

If you win, don't celebrate, and when you see your opponent, don't talk about the match: 'When the match is done, it's over. You have to move on.'

Nicolas Mahut, who lost a marathon match to John Isner at the 2010 Wimbledon Championships, on 'HOW TO BE FRIENDS WITH YOUR RIVALS' ...

It's possible to become friends with a player after they have beaten you: 'For example, I became friends with John Isner after our 11-hour match at the 2010 Wimbledon Championships. Although I lost, that match will always remain very special for both of us. I'm always going to be a part of tennis history, and I'm proud of that, and I'm working hard every day to experience such great moments. Since that match, John and I have become real friends and we now share much more than tennis. I am the first person to be happy for him for every success he gets and I am sure he is for me as well. That means a lot to me.'

As a young player, you have to be more careful about protecting yourself – you shouldn't tell your rivals and friends too much about your tennis and what you're thinking: 'Of course, this depends on the friendship you think you have with your rival. But, ultimately, tennis is an individual sport, and you have to think about yourself, and how you are trying to find success.'

Try to focus on your game, and not pay any attention to your opponent: 'Competing against a friend on court is not an easy thing. But we are first and foremost tennis players and competitors.'

Tennis is an individual sport, but it's definitely a plus to have friends on the tour and to feel support: 'Every player has his own team, his coach, his physio and more. But, because of all the time we spend together on the tour, it's natural to form friendships with other players.'

> 'It's natural to form friendships with other players.'
> **NICOLAS MAHUT**

Sergiy Stakhovsky, who defeated **Roger Federer** in the second round of the 2013 Wimbledon Championships, **on 'HOW TO PLAY AGAINST THE TOP PLAYERS'** ...

Don't make the mistake of thinking your opponent is superhuman: 'Many players don't believe in themselves as they leave the locker-room. I know it's hard to believe when you play Roger Federer at Wimbledon or when you play Rafa Nadal at Roland Garros because they are outrageously good. I was trying not to think about the fact I was playing Federer at Wimbledon. I didn't want to keep thinking, "I'm playing Roger, I'm playing Roger." When someone who is lower-ranked than you plays a great shot, you think to yourself, "Oh, that was lucky." And then when Federer produces the same shot, you think, "Oh, that was great, that's Roger." Try to remember that your opponent is just a human being, and he is also going to miss, and he is also going to make mistakes, so you need to play your game and see what he plays.'

As you walk on court, you need to be ready to fight: 'I never go into a match against the big guys sure that I'm going to win it. I go on court thinking, "I'm going to fight," and if I fight hard enough, I'll have a chance.'

Make your opponent play his shots. Don't be stupid and give him anything for free: 'If your opponent is going to win a match, he's going to have to earn it by hitting winners. And hitting winners isn't easy.'

Lukas Rosol, who defeated **Rafa Nadal** in the second round of the 2012 Wimbledon Championships, for what was one of the greatest shocks in tennis history, **on 'HOW TO CAUSE AN UPSET'** ...

Just relax and play. If you're playing a seeded opponent, you have nothing to lose. Your seeded opponent is the guy who will feel stressed and under pressure: 'You have to believe in yourself, don't get stressed and then you will play good tennis. When I played against Rafa, I was under no pressure.'

If you do cause an upset, savour the moment, but you need to build on that success: 'I've only ever watched the match against Rafa a couple of times, and just the fifth set, and only because my friend said, "Hey, look at this." It was funny to see it again. That was a great match against Rafa. But that's history and just one match, and I have to believe that I can have more great results.'

Victoria Azarenka, a multiple grand slam champion and a former
world No. 1, **on 'WAYS TO RELAX AND PREPARE FOR MATCHES'** ...

Dance and have some fun before going on court: 'A few years ago, I was at
a stage in my life when I hadn't been having that much fun, so music helped
me to relax before the match, and to allow me to do what I wanted to do.
That kind of became a routine.'

Choose the music that makes you feel good – that gives you energy, or
brings back good memories: 'I'm not so superstitious that, if I'm playing
well, I have to listen to the same music before every match. I would listen
to whatever makes me feel good, or whatever gives me the best energy, or
brings back good memories, as listening to music really helps to bring back
good memories. Before I walked on court to win the 2012 Australian Open,
I was listening to Beyoncé, and before the 2013 Australian Open I was
listening to a compilation which my boyfriend [the pop star Red Foo] had
made for me.'

Only do this if it works for you. You may find that you play better if you
don't listen to music: 'Don't do it just because you want to copy me. Only
do it if it genuinely makes you feel good, if the music makes you feel excited,
or makes you want to move, and takes you to the level that will allow you to
perform on court.'

Ernests Gulbis, who played in his first grand slam semi-final at the
2014 French Open, **on 'HOW TO MAKE THE MOST OF YOUR TALENT'** ...

If juniors want to be successful, they have to behave like pros, not like the
other juniors. There's no place for joking around: 'You see straight away the
difference between men's tennis and junior tennis. When you see the juniors
practising and playing, they don't take every point seriously. They allow
themselves to joke around, and they don't work hard enough. If you see the
guys on tour, especially the top guys, that doesn't ever happen on court.'

At the same time, you don't want a coach who will just bark orders: 'The
work ethic is different. A coach needs to teach the players, but not to turn
them into robots – they shouldn't just tell players to do something and the
players do it, they need to explain to the players why they are doing it. It's
about a long-term relationship. It's like being in school, it's education.'

David Ferrer, a former French Open finalist,
on 'HOW TO FIGHT FOR EVERY BALL' ...

It's important to have the right attitude: 'I always give my best and run down every ball, and never give up. You should always want to give your best, and to make your opponent fight for every ball, as you don't want to give them anything. They need to work for every point.'

You're going to need to be in great physical shape: 'If you're not in good shape, it's going to be almost impossible for you to retrieve balls.'

Look closely at your strengths and weaknesses: 'You have to look at your game, and work out how to give yourself the best chance of winning.'

Jerzy Janowicz, a former Wimbledon semi-finalist,
on 'HOW TO HAVE A BREAKTHROUGH TOURNAMENT' ...

As you wait for your breakthrough, it's important to keep motivated and focused on your goals: 'It was not long ago that I was playing at low-level tournaments so I know that success is tough to achieve. Tennis is very up and down – as a player you have to be able to adjust to winning and losing. If I am working hard towards my goals then I know the results will come naturally.'

Believe in yourself. And have people around you who believe in you, too: 'I will always remember the 2012 Paris Masters because it was one of those rare times when everything went right. I had worked very hard up until that point and I knew if I continued to focus on what I had worked on in practice that I could go a long way. My confidence grew with each match as I came through qualifying and all the way to the final. I have a really good team around me – including my coach and my family – that support me every day. They are always behind me 100 per cent and that allows me to know that I can achieve great things on the tennis court. If I'm at my best I know I can beat anyone on any given day, and that confidence comes from the team around me pushing me to be my best.'

Don't think too far ahead – it's important to stay in the moment and to take one match at a time: 'If you go into a tournament thinking about how many matches you have to win, that can get very overwhelming – that's especially true if you start in qualifying.'

The biggest mistake you can make after a breakthrough tournament is to imagine that you've made it. So keep working hard: 'You always have to remember to stay focused – don't think the journey to the top is easy. Take what you did and build on your experience one match and one tournament at a time.'

After making your breakthrough, it's important to set new goals: 'Be sure to set small goals throughout the year that can eventually lead to one of your big goals.'

Use the memories of your breakthrough tournament as a way of giving you confidence for the future: 'Everyone's different, but if you find that memories of a good tournament push you to be better then that memory should always be in the back of your mind. I find myself thinking back to that great tournament in Paris, reminding myself that I'm capable of doing it again.'

Pam Shriver, who was 16 years old when she played in the US Open final, on 'HOW TO BEHAVE AFTER A BREAKTHROUGH TOURNAMENT' ...

Don't rip everything up and start again – don't make any sudden changes to your life: 'Try to keep as much as possible exactly the same as before. That one tournament has changed how people know you, and changed your profile, but it shouldn't change what you're doing and who you have around you. I think young people find change more difficult than you imagine. People think the young are flexible, but as you grow up and go through adolescence, you want some order and structure as well.'

Learn to say no: 'There are suddenly going to be so many more demands on your time, and there are going to be deals and offers and invites to consider. Everyone will want to talk to you. But you need to make sure you don't overload your schedule.'

Focus on the details: 'Concentrate on what you're doing each day, and on each practice session, and on trying to improve.'

Don't get caught up in the hype: 'I was guilty of reading too much about myself. For a while after I played in the US Open final as a teenager, there was a lot written about me outside the tennis world, and I probably got a bit caught up in that. I didn't handle everything so well. There's probably more temptation for players now to read about themselves as everything is on the internet, but you can't believe the hype. I'm not going to suggest that every young tennis player should live in a cocoon, as I don't think cocoons are the answer, but you have to make sure that you keep your focus.'

Anna Kournikova, who played in a Wimbledon semi-final at the age of 16, on **'HOW TO COPE WITH TENNIS FAME' ...**

Don't bother with a disguise in an attempt to dodge the paparazzi – that's only going to draw more attention to you: 'As a public figure, you have to realise that the paparazzi go with the territory, and you're going to have to learn to cope with people wanting to take your picture. You can avoid putting yourself in certain situations – you can still go out and enjoy yourself, but you don't have to go to the trendiest restaurants where you know there will be lots of photographers. What I do find weird is when photographers take pictures of your private time, when you're at home.'

Do as many photo shoots as you please, but keep your focus: 'People always used to say that I was doing too much off the court. But I only ever did a lot of photo shoots when I was injured, and what else are you going to do when you're injured? I knew that I was working hard on my game, whatever anyone else was saying.'

Sometimes you have to put your fingers in your ears and ignore what people are saying about you: 'There are always going to be opinions, both good and bad, and that's OK. You have to realise that you can't please everyone. I was living my life. No one on the outside knew exactly what I was doing, what I was thinking. All that mattered to me was what I thought, and what my friends and family thought. When reading about yourself in the newspaper or online, you should only care that they got the score right, and nothing else.'

Kei Nishikori, who reached his first grand slam final at the 2014 US Open,
on 'HOW TO DEAL WITH BEING A TENNIS SUPERSTAR' ...

Keep your focus: 'Remember that you're playing for yourself, and not for anyone else; that will help you to deal with the pressure from the public.'

Goran Ivanisevic, a former Wimbledon champion,
on 'HOW TO EMBRACE YOUR SUPERSTITIONS' ...

You don't have to fight your superstitions. Have some fun with them – they are a way of relaxing your mind and stopping you from going crazy by thinking about tennis all the time: 'Every morning of the 2001 Wimbledon tournament, I would watch *Teletubbies* for 15 minutes, and every evening I would eat the same meal at the same restaurant. For me, that wasn't such a big deal. Those routines were fun, and by doing those things, I felt much more relaxed.'

Sometimes you have to be persistent: 'When I played at Wimbledon, I always used the same shower in the locker room, and the same toilet, too. Sometimes I had to wait to use the shower or the loo, if someone was in it, but that's OK. I also didn't want to walk on the lines on the court. Sometimes I wanted to use the same ball, or at the changeover I didn't get up from the chair until the other guy stood up – I waited. But that's just something to occupy your mind as otherwise you go crazy. I don't think it's a bad thing. It's fun. For me, I relax like that. Everyone relaxes in different ways.'

Anything you can do which helps you to relax is going to help you play better tennis: 'During the changeovers, I liked to look at the crowd, and see who was sitting there. I knew everybody who was sitting there. That was calming. I don't know why. It's thinking about something else rather than tennis. You need to really concentrate for three or four hours, so doing these things is a way of soothing your mind a little bit.'

Marin Cilic, who won his first grand slam title at the 2014 US Open, when he was being coached by his hero, **Goran Ivanisevic,** on 'HOW TO LEARN FROM YOUR IDOL' ...

You don't have to copy everything they do – everyone is different: 'Lots of kids in Croatia were copying Goran Ivanisevic with how he destroyed rackets. And it's true that he sometimes had some negative emotions on court, and the kids were copying that. But that worked for Goran – that was part of his personality and his charisma on court, and sometimes it helped him to play better tennis. I'm different to Goran. I'm maybe a little calmer. There were times in the past when I got negative and maybe I lost a little bit of my focus, so I always try to be as positive as I can. So even though it's great to have an idol, you should remember that you're different.'

Try to copy their work ethic – they wouldn't have got to where they are without passion and hard work: 'Goran was always my hero so when I met him as a teenager that was the biggest thing that ever happened to me. I learned so much from listening to him, and from practising with him, and seeing how he did things.'

Use their words as inspiration: 'It was a great feeling when Goran said that he could see something in my game, and that he thought I had the talent to go a long way in tennis, to reach the top. That was amazing to hear.'

COPING WITH ADVERSITY

Jonny Marray, a Wimbledon doubles champion, on 'HOW TO KEEP GOING DURING THE HARD TIMES' ...

The most important thing is that you believe in yourself and your game, and you think that you can have success as a tennis player: 'So don't let others knock the stuffing out of you. The only opinion that matters is yours. If you've got the belief, then you can be successful. I've had some hard times in my career when I've wondered whether I should stop playing, but I kept on playing because I felt as though I could achieve more on court.'

Recognise that it can be a long road to success. Patience is important. And so is perseverance: 'Since winning Wimbledon, I've had cards and letters telling me that I've been an inspiration, as I've shown that perseverance pays off and you get your reward at the end.'

Have a clear goal: 'There were times in my career when I was just floating through. You need a goal, and you also need a clear plan for how you're going to achieve that goal. Every time you go on court, you will have a clear idea of what you need to do to improve. A tennis player needs direction if they're going to be successful.'

You can't do this on your own: 'So surround yourself with good people who are going to encourage you when times are tough. They should know when it's the right moment to have a word in your ear. It was especially tough for me when I was out with an injury, and so wasn't earning anything for months, and you need that cash coming in to survive. Without my friends and family, it would have been difficult to have kept going.'

Andy Murray's former coach Mark Petchey,
on 'HOW TO DEAL WITH AN OPPONENT'S CHEATING AND GAMESMANSHIP' ...

Cheating in junior tennis is rife. But you shouldn't accuse someone of cheating after one bad line-call or even a couple: 'Only after several bad line-calls, and obviously bad ones, and if you're sure, should you say something.'

Sometimes, drastic action is needed: 'Parents are loath to teach their children to do what an opponent is doing to them, but sometimes only drastic action works. You see people getting fed up with their opponent's cheating and catching an opponent's serve on a big point and calling "out" and there's not very much that the opponent can do about it. That sends out the message to your opponent, "Are we going to play tennis or we going to play something else?" The reality is that, in junior tennis, you probably won't have an umpire or a supervisor, and this is sometimes the only way to deal with it.'

In junior tennis, you will get players who slow everything down, who keep stopping to tie up their shoelaces, or who stall in other ways. Unfortunately, there's not very much you can do about it: 'In professional tennis, there are rules in place about not taking too much time between points. There is much more scope for gamesmanship in junior tennis.'

Dan Bloxham, head coach at the All England Club, on 'HOW TO COPE WHEN PLAYING A CHEAT' ...

Know that your cheating opponent is scared and insecure: 'A cheating opponent, someone who gives bad line-calls, is the curse of junior tennis. Unfortunately, a lot of kids are giving up because of cheating opponents. It's certainly affecting the girls. It's a big issue, a big problem. The girls get very disheartened. They see it as a personal attack. With the girls, it goes deeper, it upsets them, and they think, "What's the point?" We tell our kids they have to be stronger than the cheats, those who can't play without cheating over line-calls. We tell our kids that cheats never prosper. You can cheat your way for a certain amount of time, but you can't cheat your way into the Davis Cup squad. Eventually, they will get found out.'

Don't lose your cool. Put your hand up to alert the referee to the problem: 'The referee will often ask the players to go back to the point they agree on. But obviously that's not great if your opponent was cheating when you had a match point. The good cheats wait for the right time to call your good shots out. They wait for a tiebreak or a major point.'

If there's no one around, you have to try to discuss this with your opponent: 'You have to front up.'

Realise that the cheat won't go home happy or satisfied, while you can: 'Why do you play tennis? To be No. 1 in the world? Yes, that's a dream. But, along the way, whichever bus stop you get off at, hopefully you've learnt to compete well, you've learnt to make friends, you've learnt to make good decisions, so really what we're talking about are the values of life. If the other guy cheats, what sort of person will he be, how successful can you see him being, and how happy will he be? Even if he wins, he's going to go home knowing that he's done the wrong thing. You'll go home happy, knowing that you've done the best you could, and that you're a better person.'

Elena Baltacha, a former British No. 1, who passed away in 2014 at the age of 30 after losing a battle with liver cancer, on 'HOW TO STAND UP FOR YOURSELF' ...

A top player will always want you to feed their ego. Always. So you can't show them any respect. Don't make eye contact: 'Don't make your opponent

feel as though you respect them, as that's what they want.
They want to beat you purely because of who they are.
So, whatever you do, don't let them.'

> 'It's real
> gladiator stuff,
> one against one.'
> ELENA BALTACHA

Let them know you're not going to roll over: 'I
remember a time I played Maria Sharapova in
Memphis once. She started her mind games before
the match – she didn't give me a proper warm-up as
she was just smacking the ball all over the place, or hitting
the ball right at me, and not giving me any rhythm. It was bang, bang, bang.
So I thought to myself, "Do you know what? I don't care who you are. I'm
not going to make any eye contact with you." Once the match started, I got a
good tempo going, and I was playing well, and so I started shouting "C'mon"
in Russian. I was screaming it. I think she was surprised by that – she didn't
think that I could speak Russian – and she realised that I wasn't giving her any
respect. So she responded by saying a few things to me in Russian. She was
cussing. She was basically saying to me, "Oh yeah, you can speak Russian, so
I'm going to throw it back at you." And I was loving that, as I'm one of those
players who gets good energy from situations like that, as it makes me more
competitive. It's real gladiator stuff, one against one. That really gets me going.
This carried on during the match, and she gave me a look when we shook
hands at the end. She beat me, but what I loved was that she knew I wasn't
going to just roll over. Some players might be really intimidated, and think to
themselves, "Oh, wow, Sharapova, she's amazing." I was never like that.'

Don't allow an opponent to intimidate you with a shoulder-bump – and
don't always wait for them to cross first when you're switching sides of
the court: 'I've never gone out of the way to start anything on court, but if
anything does happen I will always stand up for myself. I've had a player
deliberately bump my shoulder as we crossed at the net, so I turned and
just said, "Whatever, nice one." Some will take being shoulder-bumped, or
always being forced to go second when crossing the net, and they will get
deflated from it. They'll be thinking, "Oh, OK, I know my place. I'm not as
good as you, so I will wait my turn at the net." They get intimidated. Other
girls will think, "No, you're not going to do that to me. I'm not going to wait.
If we bump shoulders, we bump shoulders."'

You have to accept that sometimes trash-talking goes on – don't let it
affect you: 'Most of the time, if people are saying anything on a tennis court,

they're not insulting each other. It's about shouting "C'mon" across the net in your opponent's face.'

You have to be ready to deal with the occasional comment in the locker room or at lunch. Girls make comments to each other. They are small comments, but they are deliberate: 'Do you think to yourself, "Oh well, it's not worth it, I can't be bothered with that, as that's just pathetic," or do you stand your ground? That doesn't mean having a physical fight. But you can be hard headed and say something back to her. You won't see fights in a women's locker room – women aren't like that – but you will hear occasional arguments and chat, chat, chat.'

Having an argument could help you to play better tennis: 'Some people get so angry that they aren't able to concentrate on their tennis. But if you think that you react better by just letting everything go, then maybe that's what you should do. If you're someone like me who thinks to themselves, "That's not right," then reacting to your opponent is going to help you get up for the match.'

One tactic that players sometimes use is to call the physio on, or to leave the court to go to the loo, or to go back to the locker room to change their clothes. Unfortunately there's nothing that you can do about it: 'It's not as if the umpire can stop anyone from leaving the court to go to the loo. Gamesmanship happens at all levels of the game. It's one on one, and there's often a lot at stake.'

Annabel Croft, a former player and now TV and radio presenter,
on 'HOW TO DEAL WITH BITCHINESS IN TENNIS' ...

Don't engage with anyone who makes nasty comments: 'There were a few occasions when people said nasty things to me – quite abusive comments – but I always chose to ignore it and to rise above it. My theory has always been that you shouldn't engage. I see people engaging with those who have abused them, I just think, "Why are you doing that? Why are you showing someone that you've taken notice and that you've nibbled?" If you engage it shows that you've been hooked. Other people decide to go head on, but I've always thought that it's best not to do that. It's probably down to personality. Obviously if you're tired, you might deal with the situation a bit differently, but I can't think of any situation in which I would choose to deal with it head on.'

One way of protecting yourself is not to form friendships: 'Tennis is a highly competitive world, especially on the pro tour. There are a lot of egos on display. When you're up against a rival, you're like a couple of rutting deer. It's impossible in that situation not to have clashes of personality in certain situations. It wasn't until I came off the tour that I learned to view some of the other players as human beings. They were always enemies on the tour. You always viewed them as a potential opponent, as someone you would really want to beat. And you would get anxious about wanting to beat them. You don't want to give much away. One of the reasons I quit the tour at 21 was because you didn't have friendships on the tour. When you're on the tour, it's difficult to step back and look at the bigger picture.'

Monica Seles, a former world No. 1,
on 'HOW TO COPE WHEN THERE ARE COMPLAINTS ABOUT YOUR GRUNTING' …

Whatever happens, be true to yourself: 'All you can do as a tennis player when you go out there is to focus on yourself. You play opponents who bounce the ball 50 times before they serve, or take much longer between points than they should do, or who take injury time-outs. As long as you're not grunting to upset an opponent, it's OK.'

Realise that the better your results, and the higher you climb in the rankings, the more interest there will be in your grunting: 'I never grunted on purpose. I grunted from the age of eight. I grunted when I was ranked 83 in the world. I grunted when I was No. 1 in the world. I know that I played my heart out. That was my style of play. I can only speak for myself. I gave everything on every ball. If you look back at footage of me, when I was 12 or 14, I was grunting against the same players. But when I became No. 1, then it became an issue.'

Pam Shriver, a former US Open finalist,
on 'HOW TO DEAL WITH AN OPPONENT WHO IS GRUNTING' …

The number-one rule – and this is a pretty good life lesson – is not to let anyone upset you. Don't let someone else's behaviour or actions throw you off: 'You have to focus on yourself, and not your opponent. It's about self-care. You should be approaching every match with a clear mind. You'll probably know beforehand whether your opponent is a grunter or not, and if you're prepared for any noise that's coming, that will make it easier to deal with.'

If the noise is really extreme, if you feel as though your opponent's grunt is hindering you, and especially if you feel as though they are doing it deliberately to throw you off your game, you should appeal to them to stop: 'But ask nicely. You'll tend to get a better response if you try to appeal to their common courtesy. If that doesn't work, speak to an official, if there's one available. But there won't always be an official for amateur matches, so you are probably going to have to appeal to your opponent.'

It's important to appeal about the noise at the right time. Appeal just after you've won a game or even stop in the middle of a rally: 'But don't appeal just after you've lost a point as then it's going to look as though you're just upset about losing the point.'

Most people just play tennis for the exercise and the enjoyment, and if that's the case with you, don't organise a match against someone who you know will annoy you with their grunting: 'Of course there are going to be times when you're playing in a tournament or in a league, and you've got no choice, you're stuck with the grunter. But if you do have a choice, don't book the grunter.'

Chris Evert, a winner of 18 grand slam singles titles,
on 'HOW TO DEAL WITH NERVES' ...

Prepare before going on court: 'I always had to be on my own for an hour before a match. I couldn't socialise in the locker room. I used to listen to music, or lie down and visualise the matches, anything to get in the right frame of mind.'

Make the most of the warm-up: 'It used to take me two or three games to get into my groove. I was known for being a slow starter. So during the warm-up, I made sure that I ran around as much as possible, and got a sweat going, as then I could start properly.'

It's important to be aware of what nerves do to you physically, as then you know how to combat that: 'Some people are paralysed by nerves. They start double-faulting, or their feet feel as though they are made of lead. If you have a problem with double-faults, hit second serves on your first serve, so at least you get the ball in. If your movement suffers when you're nervous, try to stay on your toes at all times, and make exaggerated movements. Dealing with nerves came naturally to me – Martina Navratilova had the athletic genes, and I had the mental genes. I was able to stay calm.'

Stefan Edberg, a former world No. 1 who won six grand slam titles and is now coaching **Roger Federer, on 'HOW TO STAY CALM ON COURT'** ...

Think positively – the great thing about tennis is that you can play lousy shots for an hour and still win the match: 'Sometimes you have to accept that your opponent is going to do a better job than you at hitting the ball. You have to realise that there was nothing you could have done about it, and think, "OK, fine, now it's my turn to hit a great shot." It's all about psychology. There are going to be frustrations on court, but think positively. Even if you play badly for an hour, you're still in the match, remember that.'

Start to train the mind by taking a good approach to practice sessions, and that will carry over into matches: 'Sometimes it takes time to change your approach. Look at Roger Federer, he used to be more emotional on court, and he taught himself to be calmer. As you get older, you realise that tennis is very complicated – there are so many elements that go into it – and the mind is very important. You have to train the mind.'

You can learn a lot from watching players who always stay calm on court: 'I'm a naturally calm person. But when I was growing up in Sweden, we looked up to Bjorn Borg and saw how he behaved on the court, how he stayed calm and dealt with everything. You can't be someone you're not, so if you have a temper you're still going to have that temper, and you have to let it all out. But you need to control yourself.'

Simona Halep, who played in the 2014 French Open final,
on 'HOW TO AVOID FEELING STRESSED ON COURT' ...

If you're feeling too much stress on court, you need to learn to enjoy the game, and not just the results: 'When you're stressed you can't move your body, or hit the ball. I've experienced that. But if you're more relaxed on court, and you're taking pleasure from your tennis, you'll be able to play your best.'

It's important not to be too frightened or defensive – be bold and play your shots: 'I used to be frightened. So I was playing too defensively, and I was running a lot. I decided I would play more aggressively, and that I would make the points shorter.'

Marin Cilic, who won the 2012 Queen's Club title after
David Nalbandian was defaulted for injuring a line-judge,
on 'HOW TO COPE WHEN YOUR OPPONENT IS HAVING A TANTRUM' ...

Turn their negative energy into something positive – you should be encouraged by how they are behaving: 'When you look over the net and see that your opponent is losing it, that he's getting frustrated, and angry, and he's throwing his racket, that's a sign you're doing something right.'

Keep on doing what you're doing. Don't let up: 'As they say in boxing, your opponent is on the ropes. But you have to be consistent and persistent, so keep on playing the way you've been playing and hopefully you will go on to win the match. They could get fired up. You don't want to let them back into the match. You want to push the guy off the cliff.'

While you should take notice of what your opponent is doing, you can't allow yourself to be distracted: 'Don't let your mind wander. Concentrate on what you have to do. Focus on yourself. That's not always easy, of course, and the situation at Queen's Club with Nalbandian was very difficult for me.'

Goran Ivanisevic, a former Wimbledon champion,
on 'HOW TO DEAL WITH THE VOICES IN YOUR HEAD' ...

There's always a little negativity in everybody's head. You have to recognise that when you're on court for hours it's not going to be possible for everything to be beautiful and positive, all flowers and sunshine: 'You'll have some negative thoughts and some conflict in your head. I had a Good Goran and a Bad Goran. Bad Goran was influenced by the people around him, by the court, and he wanted to fight with everybody, and he wanted to leave the court. Good Goran said to Bad Goran, "Come on, it's not over yet, let's fight." It was a little chit-chat in my head. It was between points, and then, sitting on my chair, between games.'

The voices in your head don't have too much time to talk. You have to negotiate quickly: 'The problem in tennis is that everything goes so quickly in your head, from good to bad, from bad to good. Whatever you do, you have to make a quick decision, and hopefully it will be a good decision. And hopefully whatever you're thinking at that moment will be for the best. The faster you get out of that conflict, the better.'

Once you've reached a decision, stick with it: 'Two minutes later, don't start thinking, "Why did I make that decision?" That's wrong. You make that decision in the moment, and you stick with it.'

You need an emergency voice for when the bad voice takes over too much: 'You have to call 911, and you need the emergency voice to say to the bad voice, "come on, be good, let's play."'

> 'The faster you get out of the conflict, the better.'
> Goran Ivanisevic

Eugenie Bouchard, who reached her first grand slam semi-final
at the 2014 Australian Open, on 'HOW TO AVOID CHOKING' ...

Try to remember that playing tennis is supposed to be fun: 'What works for me is putting things into perspective. I just think to myself, "I'm just playing a tennis match – it's not life or death, or anything near that." It's just a game. If it's a tough battle, then that's fine, that's why you play tennis. You enjoy that.'

Don't think that you can control everything, as that will make you irritated: 'Players choke because they really want to win, and they want to control their opponent and the conditions, and those are things you can't control.'

Don't become obsessed with winning; just take the match point by point, and don't worry too much about the scoreboard: 'It's important not to think that you're closing out a match. You're just playing a point. So you're just playing one point at a time. That way, I don't worry about the score too much.'

The biggest mistake is thinking that you're about to win, and looking ahead to the future and to your next match: 'That's absolutely the worst thing to do.'

If you do find yourself choking, take deep breaths: 'You can tell you're choking when you get tight and start hitting shorter, and you're not hitting through the ball or playing nearly as well as you can. You're not as loose as you could be. Breathing is very important. Try to relax.'

Learn from your battles: 'With time and experience, it becomes easier to avoid choking. If you come through some tough, tight matches, that will give you the experience you need for the next time, as you can think to yourself, "I've been here and I can do this."'

Annabel Croft, a former world No. 21, on 'HOW TO USE THE CHANGEOVER' ...

Don't burn energy by fidgeting all the way through the changeover: 'Some players don't stop moving. They're picking up the racket on one side of the chair, then putting it down on the other, and then towelling themselves down, then rearranging their hat, then drinking some water, then fiddling with their racket again. Their eyes look this way and then that way. That's because they're looking back, and reflecting on what just happened, and then looking ahead and getting really distressed about everything.'

You have to learn how to forget. Anything

that has happened previously should be in the past and forgotten: 'And you need to – this is that great Billie Jean King line – stay in the moment. The top players are always trying to just focus on the next point, and not concern themselves with what has already happened.'

Chatting to the umpire is OK if you feel as though you want to rant and to get something off your chest: 'I suppose some people need to do that, but you're using up energy on something that has already happened. But if you don't speak to the umpire at the change of ends, you might spend the next game stressing about it.'

Don't sit there with a blank mind: 'You don't want to think too much, but you should be clear in your mind about your tactics and what you want to do in that next game.'

Martina Navratilova, arguably the greatest female tennis player of all time, on 'HOW TO AVOID BURNOUT' ...

You should always be looking to improve, as that will keep you motivated: 'I just loved the sport, and wanted to be the best tennis player that I could be. Great players always think they can do better.'

If you're trying to play as little as possible, you've probably lost some of your love for the sport. And you need a break: 'I played burnt-out tennis for a while in the 1980s, and I didn't even know it. I should have known when I was making the schedule for the following year, and I said to my coach, "How few tournaments can I play and still stay at No. 1 in the world?" That should have been the clue that I was burnt out. Had I been a psychologist, or known what I know now, I would have said to myself, "OK, you're burnt out – you need to take some time off and then come back fresh."'

If you're unsure, speak to a friend who also plays tennis: 'In 1989, I started talking to Billie Jean King, and I said, "Billie, I don't know what's going on, I'm playing but I'm struggling," and she said, "You're just burnt out – do you still love the sport?" I said, "Well ... " She said, "You need to figure that out. You need to regain the love that you had when you were a little girl hitting against the wall. If you can't feel that wonder or love, you should do something else." I took a week off, didn't do anything, and then I thought to myself, "I want to play." I played for several more years, and I loved it. I didn't take that much time off, just that one week when I did nothing. That was enough. I just needed to recharge my batteries and realise how much I loved the game. I had been playing for all the wrong reasons. I had lost sight of how much I love the game.'

Dan Bloxham, who is Master of Ceremonies for the Wimbledon Championships, and so responsible for getting the players on to Centre Court,

on 'HOW TO COPE WITH A RAIN DELAY' ...

You can't control the rain so don't bother trying: 'If you're a young player, look at the example of the top players, who just make good decisions. They come off the court, they sort themselves out, they have a shower, they do all the things they need to do. And they stay really calm. Just try to control the things that you can control. Just try to be relaxed. It's tough when you have to warm up and get ready three or four times, maybe even more, to play a match. But again, that's not something you can control.'

Try to establish with the referee how much time you have before you go back on court: 'You need to know whether you've got the time to do the things you want to do.'

If it looks as though there's going to be a long delay, don't leave it too long before eating again: 'You have to be sharp with what's going on.'

Don't spend the rain delay looking back at what has already happened in the match. Instead, you should be relaxing and thinking about what's ahead of you: 'The top players will be thinking about what they're going to be doing when they go back out. They wouldn't be reviewing how they are two sets up or how they are two sets down. If there's an hour or two, they would be relaxing. And then about 15 to 20 minutes before the match, they would start to mentally prepare themselves. They would start their build-up again.'

THE PHYSICAL GAME

GETTING IN SHAPE

Gael Monfils, who has been ranked in the world's top 10, and who is regarded by many as the best athlete in tennis, **on 'HOW TO IMPROVE YOUR FLEXIBILITY'** ...

Stretch every day – if you're not warmed up you could hurt yourself: 'I am lucky enough to be naturally flexible, but stretching every day before and after practice sessions and matches is a must. In my opinion, flexibility is important for two reasons. One is that it will help you to prevent injuries, and the other is that it will help your defensive skills. For me personally, being flexible allows me to catch balls that most players would not normally be able to reach. You also need speed to get to the ball first, but the flexibility will help you to find the right position to hit it, perhaps by doing the splits, for example. The biggest mistake you can make is to start working on your flexibility without being properly warmed up as that's the best way to get injured.'

Work on the practice court to recreate situations that you will face in a match: 'It is very important in this case to be properly warmed up before you start.'

But you don't just have to work on your flexibility on the court or in the gym: 'I would suggest going to some yoga and hip-hop classes to work on different parts of your body. Those new moves will improve your flexibility and help you in match situations.'

If you're stiff, and need to do a lot of work on your flexibility, you have to start slowly: 'You should not start too hard but try to go progressively and do a bit more every day; this way you will gain flexibility. The routine for a stiff player should be different to the routine for someone who has better flexibility. There is no need to push yourself too much one day and not be able to do anything the next day. Flexibility training needs to happen every day, step by step with the intention of doing a little more every day.'

Be aware that doing the splits at full speed carries a risk – save the splits for the big moments in matches: 'I would try to avoid doing the splits, especially at full speed. Doing the splits is very demanding for the body and there is always the risk of injury. Even when I'm on the practice court, I try to keep them to a minimum. I like to save myself for the big moments in a match. I always think that this one ball that I will get could make the difference in the end.'

Andre Agassi's fitness trainer, Gil Reyes, on 'HOW TO GET IN SHAPE FOR TENNIS' ...

Agassi achieved the career golden slam, winning all four majors and the Olympics.

If you're going to be successful you're going to need strong legs. 'At every level of the sport, including amateur level, players are hitting the ball harder. What that means is you're going to have to be able to retrieve and get to a faster ball. And that, of course, puts everything on the legs, everything. Whether you've just taken up the sport, or you're an aspiring player, you also have to work on your lower back, and on your shoulders and wrists, but they are all secondary to the legs.'

If you're working with a physical trainer or coach, communication is so important – tell the trainer how you feel on the court, and how you want to feel. And the trainer needs to listen: 'Andre was a teenager when we started working together. He was so clear with me. He said:

"Make me strong and I can win." Everyone knew that Andre was a great tennis player; he just needed to become a more complete athlete. I needed to learn from Andre what it was that he wanted out there. So he taught me, and then he relied on me to put it into a plan for him, and to do it safely, because he didn't have a background in weightlifting. That communication led to an amazing relationship that still exists today. We made it through an entire career.'

Don't be in a rush. Start slowly: 'That could just be a light jog around the block. The weekend warrior's lament is starting too fast. It's much better to think that you didn't do enough, as you can easily correct that. Unfortunately, if you do too much at the beginning you might end up with a problem that could set you back weeks or even months. Young players see the extraordinary athleticism on the tour, and they're in a rush to get into the gym and start lifting weights that can cause a wave of injuries. Tennis wasn't previously associated with weightlifting and now it is. Sometimes the enthusiasm, the zeal, will create problems. That concerns me greatly.'

Squats are the best and the worst exercise ever invented by man: 'After starting slowly, you then want to strengthen your legs. But you must do that safely. I happen to be one of those who loves squats. But there's so much potential for injury to the knees and lower back.'

It's important to strengthen your lower back: 'Whenever you play a shot – especially a serve, but also with your groundstrokes – you're generating torque, and that comes from your lower back and your abdominals.'

As well as building strength, you need to demonstrate it: 'Andre running up the hills was a follow-up to our strength training. Andre felt as though running the hills was something he had to do to challenge his leg strength. Running the hills wasn't about getting his legs stronger; it was a measure of where he was at any given point. That was him saying to me, "Keep on pushing me, keep on getting me stronger."'

Martina Navratilova, a winner of 18 grand slam singles titles, on 'FITNESS FOR TENNIS' ...

Don't just play tennis – do other sports, such as football, basketball and track and field, for cross-training: 'That will give you a different perspective of what you're doing geometrically on the court, as well as using the body a little differently. If you just play tennis, you could end up with more physical issues.'

Players now spend too much time in the gym when they should be doing more physical work on the court: 'Do drills on the court that are very physical because then, at the same time as getting in shape, you're also learning how to play.'

Strength training will help you maintain control over your shots: 'You want to be able to hit the ball just as hard in the final set as you did in the first set. When you lose power, you lose control. If you have to use more power to swing just as hard, you're going to miss more.'

To avoid boredom, work on something different every day: 'There's always plenty to improve.'

Keep track of what you are doing on the practice court – that trains the mind: 'Count everything. A lot of times, players will just hit, hit, hit. They miss three balls in a row and think "no big deal", and don't change anything. And then you play a match and miss three balls in a row it's 0–40. Whoops. So when you do drills count to 11 or 20. And practise match situations, which means playing sets.'

If you're going to serve and volley, or attack the net a lot, you have to be in excellent shape: 'The type of game I played, you had to be in really good shape. I don't just mean endurance; I played a very explosive type of game, so that takes a lot more out of you than just staying on the baseline and running from side to side. It takes a lot more energy running forward and back rather than side to side. Side to side you can do all day long. But running up and down, you need to be in great shape to do that.'

Gil Reyes, who worked for 17 years as
Andre Agassi's strength and conditioning trainer,
on 'HOW TO WORK ON YOUR FITNESS DURING THE OFF-SEASON' ...

You'll need a physical and mental break after a long season, but it's important that you don't let yourself get out of shape: 'The off-season should be the time when you do your toughest training.'

To counter the problems of wear-and-tear, you need to keep your body in tip-top shape. Whether you're a competitive or a recreational player, use the off-season to build up your strength and it will increase your enjoyment of playing tennis: 'Think about how many times a player starts and stops, starts and stops, in every point – that's jarring and jolting and putting a beating on your knees, your lower back, your hips, your ankles. So you have to keep your body strong.'

Madison Keys, a US tennis star, on 'HOW TO FUEL YOURSELF FOR TENNIS' ...

Try to avoid getting stuck in a routine during the tournament, as otherwise you will end up eating the same food in the same restaurant all week: 'If I go to the same restaurant two days in a row, I feel as I though I have to stick with the same routine and go there for the rest of the tournament. So on the second day I always try to go somewhere different so I don't get stuck in a routine.'

It's very important not to eat a big meal just before going on court: 'If you get the timing wrong, it's not going to be fun. I would suggest having a snack about half an hour before you go on court.'

Avoid foods such as pizza, cake and ice cream: 'On the day of the match, and also the night before, you should be eating proteins and carbohydrates.'

During the match, eat and drink during every changeover: 'Every time I sit down, I drink something with electrolytes in it, and I take a bite of something, whether it's a banana or an energy bar.'

After the match, drink some water and a recovery shake, and then have lunch or dinner.

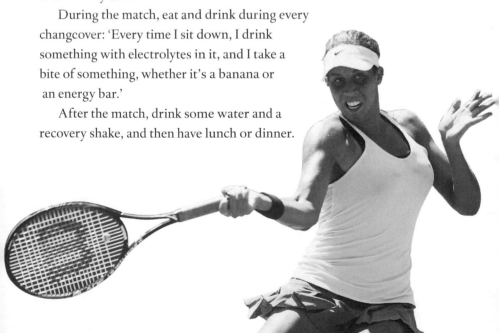

Leander Paes, a former doubles world No. 1,
on 'HOW TO IMPROVE YOUR REFLEXES' ...

Play video games: 'When I was a kid, my dad gave me 100 rupees a day to play video games. He realised that when I was looking at a screen, I would be really working on my hand-eye coordination.'

Play tennis against your garage wall: 'Don't do it against your living room wall, as your mum won't be pleased. Go outside and just go bang, bang, bang with the ball against the wall. And go forehand-backhand, forehand-backhand. And then after that you go low forehand-high backhand, low backhand-high backhand. You basically work the different reflexes. Start off by standing ten feet from the wall, then you go to eight feet from the wall and then you go to five feet from the wall. And then three feet. By the time you get to three feet away, it's bang, bang, bang, bang. It's very quick. It's like a boxer working on a punchbag. You're building up muscle memory, as well as building up your forearm muscles.'

You can also do the wall practice with a football: 'This helps your eye-foot co-ordination and reflexes – people seem to forget about that.'

Heather Watson, a former junior US Open champion,
on 'HOW TO IMPROVE YOUR MOVEMENT' ...

Push yourself so hard that you're almost in tears: 'This sport is just 10 per cent talent – the rest is hard work – and you will have to apply yourself to improve your movement. I do lots of running drills, side to side and back and forth, and while I've never felt sick, I have sometimes felt as though I'm about to cry my eyes out. I'm working so hard, both mentally and physically, and I'm trying to push through.'

Run on the beach: 'Running in the sand is very good for your legs. It's especially tough when you do it at 7am, and you know that you've got a full day of weights and tennis ahead of you. But you need to train hard.'

'Running in the sand is very good for your legs.'
HEATHER WATSON

Kei Nishikori, who reached his first grand slam final at the 2014 US Open, on 'HOW TO MAKE SPEED YOUR WEAPON'...

First you must recognise that speed can be a weapon in tennis. If you can run down a lot of balls, you can hurt your opponent: 'I have to be fast around the court because I'm not the biggest guy on the tour. So speed has become my biggest weapon.'

> 'A trainer can teach you how to run correctly.'
> KEI NISHIKORI

When you do your drills, you should replicate your movement in matches: 'In matches you'll be running to get a ball, and then you'll be trying to get into position before chasing another ball down. Those are the movements you should be making in training.'

There are different running skills – running forwards, running backwards and running sideways – and you need to work on all of them: 'Some people are good at running side to side, but aren't so good going forwards and backwards, or vice versa, and then you have a weakness.'

Don't assume that you know how to run properly – you might need to change your running style: 'I worked with a trainer who taught me how to run correctly.'

Sloane Stephens, who reached her first grand slam semi-final at the 2013 Australian Open, **on 'HOW TO BE A GREAT ATHLETE'** ...

Appreciate that being in good shape will give you a psychological and mental edge: 'Fitness leads to better stamina, quickness, and heavier balls. Fitness also affects the mental side of the game. Going into every match, I believe I am in better shape than my opponent. That gives me an advantage before the match even begins, as I have the confidence to play my best.'

Becoming a better athlete takes a lot of sacrifice and hard work, so you'd better make sure you love it: 'To become a better athlete, you need to spend a lot of time on the court, and on the track and in the gym. I spend between 7 and 10 hours a week on physical fitness, and I truly feel it makes a big difference to my game.'

Stretch before and after you train or play if you want prevent injury: 'Dynamic stretching is really good for warming up. It gets the blood flowing and stretches out the muscles at the same time. After matches, I recommend static stretching. This really cools the muscles down and gets the lactic acid out, which causes soreness.'

Ice after training: 'This is the hardest part of my fitness regime – it's so cold – but how you recover after training is as important as the training itself. I know how important this is, so I suck it up. I always feel way better afterwards, too.'

Fuel your body: 'I try to stick to protein and carbs in the morning so I have energy for practice. I eat a big lunch so I can refuel my body for my next practice. It is very important to put some food in your body within an hour of when you finish training. And I try not to eat dinner too late, before 6pm if possible.'

STAYING IN SHAPE

Caroline Wozniacki, a former world No. 1, on 'HOW TO STAY FIT ALL YEAR' ...

You can't just rely on your pre-season training – that only gives you your fitness base for the first half of the season: 'Halfway through the year, I take a break from competition and work hard on my fitness and then I'm fit for the rest of the year.'

It's hard to stay disciplined throughout the year, so if you can, work out with a trainer: 'I have a fitness guy with me on the tour. I think it's good to have someone there because to do it yourself all the time is not easy.'

Keep working out alongside your tennis: 'You can go to the gym during tournaments but it depends if you have matches, how tough it's been, if you have days off or not. Sometimes it's just balance work, sometimes it's core exercises or back work, sometimes it's a longer session, but it depends on how you feel.'

We use the core for everything so keep it strong: 'The big muscles in the core need to be strong, but so do the small muscles around them because they are the ones that can tear, especially on the serve if you make a wrong movement. So those are the ones that are extra important to work on because if your core is strong everything you do on the court will be stronger too.'

Listen to your body: 'It's OK to sometimes drop a tournament if you feel tired.'

Sam Stosur, a former US Open champion,
on 'HOW TO MAINTAIN YOUR FITNESS DURING THE YEAR' ...

Just playing matches isn't enough you also have to do off-court work: 'The goal during the year is obviously to play lots of matches, and the more matches you play, the less training you have to do. But you still have to do off-court work, with players at all levels getting faster and stronger.'

You're not really grinding it out, as you would during the off-season; during the season, it's about topping up: 'There are similarities between off-season and in-season training – it's probably just the volume that's different. During the season, the off-court training isn't as physically demanding. During the off-season, you're building up everything and getting a base. During the season, the work you do is probably a bit more specific – there will be an area you want to work on.'

Try to do a training block around the middle of the season: 'I do a training block after Wimbledon for a couple of weeks. I'll also do a week here and a week there throughout the year, depending on how I do at tournaments.'

A typical in-season training day would involve a bit of time on court, maybe between one and two hours: 'If I've got maybe three or more days before I play a match, I'll do a gym session to work on my strength, or a cardio session. But otherwise just exercises – they're not so physically demanding, but you're looking after your body, and staying on top of things. You've also got to think about nutrition, and being healthy. I try to have a massage about once a week.'

Don't forget to rest. This can be overlooked a lot, especially when you're younger: 'You don't have a day off for weeks on end, and then you break down and you get injured. Sometimes it's just as important to be resting and recovering as to be training. So get in the pool, or if there's a beach nearby, get in the water. You've got to have your days off. During a training block, you've got to have rest – at least one day a week – as otherwise you're going to be wrecked.'

Andrea Petkovic, who has been ranked in the world's top 10, on 'HOW TO WARM UP FOR MATCHES' ...

You want to be sweating before you go on court – getting your legs and your footwork going will help you to get rid of pre-match nerves: 'Right before I go on court I do a lot of quick steps and short sprints.'

Simulate playing tennis: 'You're swinging, you're playing the strokes, you're playing shadow tennis. That focuses your mind that you're going to play a match, and you're imagining the strokes you're going to play, including the technique. This has helped me tremendously – since I started doing this, I haven't had as many slow starts as I used to.'

Warming up is boring, but don't skip it: 'Even though I hate warming up – it's the worst part of my job – it's so important to do it. I hate it because it's so boring, because I've been doing the same routine for years. But I zone out, and maybe do things automatically because I've done them so many times before. Warming up helps you to avoid injuries, especially when you're tight and you really want to win, as then the muscles get a little smaller so you have to make sure each muscle in your body is ready to go.'

While your warm-up needs to be intense, you don't want to do so much that you tire yourself out: 'And don't go running around like a crazy maniac. I usually do 10 to 12 minutes, and that's after I've practised earlier. Sometimes the matches before yours go on for longer than you thought, and maybe it's two, three or four hours since you practised, and then it's necessary to warm up for 20 minutes to get your body ready. Your body has to know it's now time to perform. You're sending your body and mind a message: "Be prepared, and don't get injured."'

> **'Don't go running around like a crazy maniac.'**
> ANDREA PETKOVIC

Coco Vandeweghe, who has been ranked in the world's top 50, on 'HOW TO WARM DOWN' ...

Figure out a routine that works for you and then do it every single time, after every match, whether you've won or lost: 'Some players, when they lose a match, just want to get the heck out of there. They just think "forget it". But I think that if you stick to that same routine, it's going to help calm yourself down if you're elated after a win. Or if you're disappointed after a defeat, you can use that routine as an opportunity to collect yourself if you're not as stable as you want to be. By doing the routine, you're going to be ready to face all the things you need to face after a match. It's mental as well as physical. It would be a mistake to do nothing, to skip a warm-down. The warm-down is as important as the warm-up, especially when you are still in the tournament.'

Start your routine as soon as you come off court – don't do anything else until you have warmed down properly: 'I start with 10 minutes on an exercise bike, at a low-level intensity, to flush through the legs. Then I do an ice bath. Then, if I have a day off before I play my next round, I have a massage. But if I'm playing the next day, I don't have a massage as I feel heavy-legged the day after a massage. I do a good stretch in the evening, 30 minutes minimum.'

If you've had a tough match, you might want to have some food straight away: 'I like a simple carbohydrate as my stomach won't be quite ready for anything else. After dinner, I'll drink my protein drink – which also contains carbohydrates – before I go to bed.'

Victoria Azarenka and Andy Murray's former chiropractor, Jean-Pierre Bruyere, on 'HOW TO RECOVER AND COOL DOWN AFTER MATCHES' ...

Drink a pint of beer: 'Studies have shown that drinking beer can help you. Beer is a diuretic so it helps to clean out your system. But it has to be non-alcoholic beer, as you can't get drunk after a match. So you don't have to stick to traditional sports drinks. I also recommend chocolate milk – at one stage, Victoria was drinking that, and she loved it.'

Don't think you need to eat six chickens as soon as you walk off court: 'If you've just played for five hours, then, yes, you have to fuel yourself. But if you've only been on court for 90 minutes, there's no need to eat so quickly.'

After a long match, one of the best things you can do is just walk around – this could stop you from passing out: 'If you suddenly stop moving, your heart will slow down and your blood goes to your legs and feet, and that can make you feel dizzy.'

Have an ice bath – it won't feel great when you're in there, but it will do when you get out: 'This is especially true if you've been playing somewhere hot, like Australia – getting in the ice bath will help to lower your body temperature.'

Although it's good to stretch, you don't have to do it straight away – just so long as you do it within two hours of the match finishing: 'It's best to do it when you're relaxed, and when you don't have people around you. It's a chance for you to see where the tensions are in your body, and where you're tight, and to see whether you need to have any extra treatment to your body.'

Don't do things for the sake of it: 'There's not much science behind cool down routines, and with some coaches and physical trainers I think it's a case of wanting to be seen to be doing something. I think that's totally wrong. Players get so used to doing the same routine, but perhaps they need to look carefully at what they're doing, and to think about whether the routine is helping them to recover.'

INJURIES

Wayne Ferreira, who played in 56 consecutive grand slams, on 'HOW TO AVOID SERIOUS INJURY'...

While you need to be flexible and supple, with big, strong legs, having a big upper body can be hard on the legs as you're carrying that extra weight around the court: 'Tennis is legs and core based. If you have good stomach muscles, and good strong legs, you don't really need a strong upper body.'

Don't try to play through any injury – take some time off: 'When you have an injury in one part of your body, you'll overcompensate in other parts of your body, and everything starts going off.'

As a teenager, you have to be really careful when you're going through a growth spurt, so don't overdo the weightlifting: 'Somebody who is 14, 15, 16 years old shouldn't be lifting too many heavy weights. When your body is still growing, that can be quite damaging. I would suggest using bands, and the low weight and high repetition stuff, and only start bench-pressing and all that sort of stuff when you are fully-grown. That's probably when you're 18 or 19.'

It's OK to drink the occasional beer, but you need a healthy diet: 'I never snacked, or ate junk food. And I always tried to eat healthily, but I don't think you need to be very strict.'

Take any opportunity to have a full body check-up: 'Then you'll know where your strengths and weaknesses are, and which areas you need to build up.'

Work hard at being in the best physical shape you can be: 'Do as much maintenance on your body as you can. Work hard at preventative care. Take a massage after every match. Stretch before and after matches and training sessions.'

Jean-Pierre Bruyere
on 'HOW TO AVOID INJURIES WHEN PLAYING ON GRASS' ...

Grass is probably the most dangerous surface on which to play tennis – if you don't feel safe, stop at once: 'Also, the actual surface differs quite considerably from one part of the court to the other – the grass will be worn down the most at the baseline – and this makes it dangerous. If there's any moisture on the court, you have to be really careful. I think players get injured because they just think they should continue, and no one has told them to stop. You need to make a decision yourself and to tell the umpire that it's too dangerous and that you want to stop. Don't think about what others want, and what they're expecting from you. It's your health, so do what you can to protect yourself.'

Don't go 'cold' into playing a match on grass – practise on the surface first so your muscles can get used to it: 'I wouldn't advise on making too many changes to your physical fitness routine off the court. I think you get the most benefit from actually being on the court, and getting a feel for the grass again. That will allow your body to adapt to the experience. If you go straight into a match, you're going to end up feeling very tight.'

Don't think about playing on the lawns without special grass-court shoes: 'You'll slide all over the place and you might hurt yourself.'

To play well on grass, you need to spend as much time as possible getting low, so you need to have strong glute muscles: 'This is especially true if you are playing on a grass court that isn't being used for professional tennis – the bounces on amateur courts tend to be much lower. You need to lower your centre of gravity and get used to bending your knees. You also need to strengthen your back and your legs, especially if there is a problem with your footing. Cardiovascular isn't as important on grass as it is on other surfaces, because you can win more points with your serve, and the rallies don't go on so long.'

Jean-Pierre Bruyere
on 'HOW TO AVOID TENNIS ELBOW' ...

It's important that the grip is the right size, and that you don't hold it too hard.

Don't sit hunched over a computer all day: 'If you're on the computer the whole time, that could cause issues with your shoulder. And if you have problems with your shoulder, all the power will have to come from the wrist and the elbow, and that could lead to tennis elbow.'

Ask a coach to look at your technique and to tell you whether anything needs to be corrected.

If you are in any pain or discomfort, don't try to play through it – seek medical advice.

Gil Reyes
on 'HOW TO DEAL WITH CRAMP' ...

To avoid getting cramp in the first place, make sure you're properly hydrated. However, just replacing the water you're losing isn't enough – you also have to replace the minerals, electrolytes and enzymes that you lose as you perspire: 'You can do that by eating fruits and vegetables, with bananas and potatoes high in the potassium you need to stop you from cramping. You should also consider taking a mineral supplement.'

Once you have cramp, your body is sending out a pretty urgent signal, and there's not much you can do about it, but you could try gently rubbing or stretching your muscle: 'Realistically, there's very little that you can do to salvage your tennis match. Once you're cramping, it's not completely futile, but it's pretty close. At that point, you're pretty much done – that seems to be the history of it.'

Sabine Lisicki, a former Wimbledon finalist,
on 'HOW TO STAY CHEERFUL AND POSITIVE WHEN YOU'RE INJURED' ...

Don't watch tennis if it's going to be too painful for you: 'When I've been injured, I've found it too hard to even watch tennis on TV. Missing Wimbledon one year was a real heartbreaker and I knew that if I watched it I would just want to be out there on the court even more.'

Surround yourself with good people – you can't always do this on your own and you need their encouragement: 'Even during the times I have been injured, I never thought about quitting. That's because tennis is my passion and it's what I want to do. But, of course, there were days during my rehab when it was difficult and it seemed like a long way back. But those are the times when you need to have good friends and people around you who can help you stay cheerful.'

Learn to appreciate your health again: 'There was a time when I was on crutches and I had to learn how to walk all over again. That gave me a new appreciation of what it is to have two healthy legs and what it is you can do with them.'

Even if you can't play tennis, that doesn't mean you can't be competitive: 'If you can't walk or run, perhaps you can swim. During one rehab, I did a lot of swimming and I did it competitively as I was always testing myself. I wanted to improve my technique and to get better times.'

Be patient: 'One of the hardest things is knowing when you're ready to come back. I've made the mistake in the past of coming back too soon when I wasn't quite ready. That comes down to experience, of knowing what your body is capable of. And when you do come back, you have to think that you're starting from scratch again. Things are going to happen slowly so you can't expect too much at the beginning.'

Rafa Nadal's uncle and coach, Toni, on 'HOW TO APPROACH A COMEBACK FROM INJURY' ...

(Nadal's return from injury in 2013 was the greatest comeback in tennis history.)

The most important thing is the mind, because when you have a strong mind you will have a strong body and you can play strong shots: 'Without a strong mind, it's very difficult. When you're coming back from injury, it's even more important to have a strong mind. Ever since Rafa was young, when he was a boy, I have worked his mind so he can be mentally strong.'

It's easier to deal with an injury and a setback if you accept that things don't always go your way: 'In this life, things don't always go as you want. You should know that some things come good and others things not so good. That's normal in life. It's easier when you know you're going to have ups and downs in life. If you think things are always going to go well, and you never expect there to be any problems, then you're going to find life difficult.'

It's normal to have doubts when you return to competition, and when you're unsure what's going to happen: 'And when you've had a big injury, the doubts are bigger. For me, this is all very normal to have doubts. Rafa had doubts when he came back. Only people who aren't intelligent don't have doubts.'

If necessary, make some changes to your game: 'On his return, Rafa thought that he didn't want to run as much as he did before, so he started to play a bit more aggressively so the rallies were shorter.'

> 'Only people who aren't intelligent don't have doubts.'
> **TONI NADAL**

Accept that, as you get older, it gets a little harder: 'When Rafa had an injury in 2004, and missed three months, it was not so difficult. He improved, and then he came back and played, not a problem. A few years on, when he was a little older, the comeback was more difficult because you know that your body's not so young any more.'

Brian Baker, who returned to the tour after five operations, on 'HOW TO HAVE A SUCCESSFUL COMEBACK FROM INJURY' ...

Get on track mentally: 'The easiest thing in the world is to get frustrated, to get down in the dumps. You can keep on saying, "Why me? Why me?" What you need to be doing is thinking about how you are going to get back on the court.'

Your body is in a weakened state, and to get back to where you want to be, you're going to have to deal with pain, which includes learning to recognise different types of pain: 'There's tolerable pain. There's a kind of good pain that you can work through. And there's bad pain, when you have to stop.'

Resist any pressure to come back too early: 'You have to listen to your body. Some players are going to come under pressure to come back because of their contracts with sponsors, or because of the pressure from someone inside their group. But you must only come back when you're ready. Tennis is such a physical sport, so if you're not ready, you're going to hurt yourself.'

You need the support of your friends and family: 'No one ever made a successful comeback on their own. That's just impossible. What you need is their support and encouragement. It's helpful if they don't put any extra expectation on you.'

You need something else in your life to help keep your mind off your injury and rehab. Otherwise you could go crazy: 'And if it all gets too much for you, if it really upsets you, you could end up waving the white flag.'

There are going to be nerves when you play your first match back – and it will take a while to get back to your best: 'You can do all the rehab, but it's very different, mentally and physically, when you're on the match court. At the beginning there will generally be no outside pressure when you play that match. Only if you do well will the outside pressure build.'

TACTICS AND STRATEGY

Boris Becker, who won his first Wimbledon title at the age of 17, and who went on to win two more titles at the All England Club, **on 'HOW TO PLAY ON GRASS' …**

Bend your knees: 'This is the number one thing. You move on grass totally differently to any other surface. It's very slippery, very soft, and the ball bounces quite low. So therefore, whether you like it or not, you have to bend your knees at all times. The first couple of days, you're going to feel it in your legs much more than on any other surface.'

Understand the movement of the ball: 'On grass, the bounce is softer, meaning that it's slower. On clay courts and hard courts, you sometimes play behind your opponent, as you want to go against play. On grass, you want your opponent to run into the open court because the ball slides away from him, and the player, once he gets to the ball, is likely to slip on the grass. You want your opponent to move.'

Shorten the points – players don't do this enough: 'A drop shot on grass is deadly. Coming to net will also shorten the points. Most baseliners are uncomfortable with the net. But if you have any feel or understanding of how to win quicker points you will know you must come forward on a grass court. A lot of players play on grass the same way that they play on clay or on hard courts, and that's why you have such long rallies. You don't have to serve and volley. But you can still come to net.'

Virginia Wade, Britain's last female Wimbledon singles champion, on 'GREAT SHOTS TO PLAY ON GRASS' ...

Hit a lot of slices: 'The ball really shoots through, so this can be a very effective shot, especially in the first few days of a tournament when the courts will be softer and the bounce lower.'

Go easy on the kick second serves – add some variety: 'I would suggest hitting more slice serves to keep the ball down. On grass, you don't get away with hitting a basic kick second serve, as the ball will sit up to be hit. It's playing right into your opponent's hands.'

The one thing you shouldn't keep on trying to do on grass is to run around your backhand: 'Give that up. Some players are always going to be looking for that opportunity, but it's not often that you'll have time.'

Play the ball as early as you can: 'You can think that the ball is coming slowly towards you, then it bounces and shoots through. So it's best to try to hit the ball as early as you can.'

Chris Evert, a winner of seven French Open titles, on 'HOW TO PLAY ON CLAY' ...

Bring your opponent to the net: 'The net is a vulnerable place to be on a clay court. I had some of my best successes against Martina Navratilova when we played on a clay court – Martina was a net-rusher and I used to bring her to the net with a drop shot or a short ball. You're vulnerable at the net on this surface, as once you've committed to moving one way it's difficult to change direction.'

If you play most of your tennis on hard courts, stand a yard further back behind the baseline: 'That means, with the higher bounce on clay, you will immediately feel more comfortable. But when there's the opportunity you should step in and be aggressive.'

You need to be able to slide into your shot and then get back into the middle of the court as quickly as you can: 'I grew up playing on clay, so I was comfortable with sliding. But those who didn't grow up on it need to spend as much time as possible on the surface, not just learning how to slide, but how to get back into position as fast as you can.'

Playing on clay isn't about hitting outright winners the whole time, but about accuracy, strategy and patience: 'It's not easy putting opponents away on clay, so you have to break your opponent down. That means you need patience, as well as accurate groundstrokes and a variety of shots. If you're playing a powerful opponent, you want them running around and constantly out of position. You have to appreciate that on clay, you're probably going to have to play three or four more shots to finish the point off. You're going to play a lot more balls than you would do on grass or hard courts where it's easier to hit outright winners.'

Borna Coric, who was 17 when he defeated **Rafa Nadal** for the first time, and 18 when he beat **Andy Murray** for the first time, on **'PLAYING ON HARD COURTS':**

Hard courts can damage your body, so prepare properly: 'To avoid injuries, I stretch for 20 minutes every day, and I warm up for 10–15 minutes, and I try to have a massage at least twice a week.'

Don't overdo the slice or topspin: 'On hard courts, you should be playing with less spin.'

Movement is key: 'You need to learn how to slide on hard courts.'

Get your first serve in: 'You want to have a big first-serve percentage.'

> **'You need to learn how to slide on hard courts.'**
> BORNA CORIC

MARIA SHARAPOVA, CAROLINE WOZNIACKI, LI NA and SLOANE STEPHENS' former coach, **Thomas Hogstedt,** on 'PLAYING ON HARD COURTS':

To excel on this surface, you need a weapon: 'A hard court is the most neutral of the surfaces, it's fair surface. You don't have bad bounces, and you will always get a good ball coming through at you. That's why it's a good surface to learn on, and it can give you a good all-round game, and to teach you how to be consistent, but ideally you want to have one strength.'

Invest in a decent pair of shoes: 'It's the most physically demanding of the surfaces, and can be tough on your knees and on your back. That's why it's important to have shoes that offer you good support.'

Ivan Ljubicic, a former world No. 3, on 'HOW TO PLAY INDOORS' ...

Be as aggressive as possible – even if sometimes you miss a lot and look silly: 'Playing indoors, you have perfect conditions – there's no wind, no sun, nothing – so you can really swing at your shots. If you sit back and wait, you will always get an opponent who gets hot. So you need to take the initiative. If you're not going to go for your shots when you're indoors, then where and when?'

Whatever you do, don't wait for your opponent to make mistakes: 'Don't play safe; don't be defensive. So, with your second serve, don't just spin it in. The guy will just smack it, especially at high levels.'

Andre Agassi and Lleyton Hewitt's former coach **Darren Cahill,** who politely turned down a job offer from **Roger Federer,** on 'PLAYING INDOORS':

Rush your opponent: 'Take time away from your opponent by consistently rushing them with a strong court position and a willingness to make progress on every short ball.'

Attack the ball: 'Don't extend a rally just for the sake of it. If there's a ball asking to be attacked, attack it.'

It's a mistake to try to hit your serve as hard as possible: 'Don't try to over-serve in conditions that suit the server. Think more about placement and accuracy and keep that first-serve percentage up. The free points will mount up.'

Andy Murray and **Laura Robson's** former coach, **Miles Maclagan,** on 'HOW TO SCOUT AN OPPONENT' ...

Be wary of drawing too many concrete conclusions from watching a player play just once: 'Players at all levels have good and bad days, days when certain shots may or may not be working. You also need to take other factors into account. Often players are a bit nervous in their first round, not quite used to the conditions and are understandably playing quite conservatively; once they get through that match they may relax and play with a lot more freedom. Who is their opponent? They may be playing a lefty or someone who hits a lot of tricky spins, making them feel awkward on that specific day, and will you pose the same problems? Conditions such as wind, temperature and court surface can also have a strong bearing on how a player plays on any given day.'

Having said that, you can often get some helpful hints quite quickly: 'Players with extreme grips probably won't like a ball coming through low and fast, someone who tosses the ball out to the right (as a righty) will possibly favour the slice serve, and players with big shots often need extra time to set up and won't like being rushed.'

The most important aspect of tactics is knowing your own game, as it is very easy to confuse yourself with too much information and trying to do things that you are not really comfortable doing: 'The top players will vary their tactics slightly but still try to stay within their game style, using their strengths. However, there will be times when you may need to go out of your comfort zone if things aren't going well or your opponent is simply better than you.'

Caroline Wozniacki, a former world No. 1 and grand slam finalist, on 'HOW TO DEFEND' ...

You need to recognise that attack can be a great form of defence. But be patient: 'The mindset should be that you're trying to take the initiative. But don't go for crazy shots if you're not in a good position. When you're out wide in the corner of the court, don't go for a shot that you're only going to make once in every ten attempts. That's a common mistake. Instead, play the ball back deep into the court, make it back to the middle of the court and make your opponent think about what they have to do with the ball. You have to be patient. You have to wait for the right opportunity, and then go for your shot and be aggressive.'

The most important thing is to be in great shape, as you will have to retrieve lots of balls.

Playing good defence isn't about hitting the ball more softly: 'It's about playing with more spin and bigger margins over the net. And not always going so close to the lines.'

You have to adapt your defence to different surfaces: 'On grass, for example, you have to play the ball very flat and you need to be able to change the direction of the ball very quickly. On clay, the ball crosses over the net at a much greater height, and you have more time to do things. But you need to be able to slide and move well.'

Fabrice Santoro, who was known as 'The Magician' for the creative way he played with backspin, topspin and sidespin, on **'HOW TO PLAY WITH SPIN' ...**

Keep the ball on the racket for as long as possible: 'The longer you have the ball on your racket, the more control you have over where the ball will drop. It's also important to have soft hands – that will give you better feel and more time with the ball on the racket.'

Make the most of being different – keep your opponent thinking and guessing: 'These days, most tennis players will hit the ball hard from the back of the court, so most matches look the same, and they will be used to always having the same shots to play. But if you're good at using different spins and angles, and you offer something different, they are going to be uncomfortable, as they won't be used to playing an opponent like you. Don't let them settle. You want your opponent to be thinking about what you're going to do next.'

If you're playing a powerful opponent, try to keep the ball as low as possible: 'If you keep giving them balls that are around hip-height, you're going to make life easier for them – they're going to find they're very comfortable. I always found that slicing the ball and keeping it low made it tricky for them. You always have to try to make them play the ball from positions they're not used to. It's OK if they keep on hitting the ball hard: if they're in positions they're not used to, they're going to miss more. Ideally, you want to play them at your game, spin, and not at theirs, power. Play them on your terms.'

People don't realise that a good slice forehand is better than a bad topspin forehand: 'You don't have to hit a topspin forehand, just because everyone else does. I realised that my topspin forehand wasn't good enough for me to compete at the highest level, but I had a slice forehand in my pocket.'

Express yourself: 'I have never been a machine on court. Tennis was a game to me as a kid, and it remained a game when I was a professional. So have fun and use your imagination. If you use spin, you are more likely to enjoy yourself on court.'

> **'Play your opponent on your terms.'**
> **FABRICE SANTORO**

Martina Hingis, a winner of five grand slam singles titles, on 'HOW TO PLAY INTELLIGENT TENNIS' ...

Think about the geometrics: 'The closer you are to the net, the bigger the angles available to you. And when you're a long way back behind the baseline, the smaller the court gets.'

Don't keep on hitting the same shot with the same power – mess with an opponent's rhythm by mixing it up: 'You can trouble your opponent by changing the pace in rallies, or by changing the depth, playing some balls long, and then some short. Everyone these days can hit hard from the baseline. But if you can do something different, you should do it.'

Adjust to the surface you're on, and also the balls, and your opponent: 'For example, on grass, spin isn't as effective as it is on other surfaces, so you have to think about using flatter shots.'

When playing powerful opponents, a good tactic is to hit the ball back at their feet: 'Most powerful players are tall, and they won't like having to reach down low. Also, give them angles, and have them running, so they can't settle.'

Henri Leconte, a former French Open finalist, on 'HOW TO USE ANGLES' ...

Imagine you're playing chess on the court: 'To use angles, you need to have good technique, and be able to play with the ball. I mean, really play. I don't mean just hit it straight or hit it cross-court. You have to play like you're playing chess. You have to construct the point and use every angle that's possible. The best surface to work on the different shots, and to use the angles, is clay. That's because of the slower bounce. If you don't have good hands, you're not going to find this easy.'

While racket and string technology has improved, and you can now do more from the back of the court, the closer you are to the net, the easier it is to use angles: 'You will have more of the court to play with.'

Be inventive: 'I was always trying to make shots that other people weren't making. Maybe other players just didn't have the belief or talent to try things.'

Alexandr Dolgopolov, who has been ranked in the world's top 20, on 'HOW TO PLAY WITH MORE FLAIR AND VARIETY' ...

Look for opportunities to play a drop shot: 'You can't decide this before a point starts – you have to see what the situation is, and look at your court position and also your opponent's.'

Some players can win matches by being solid from the baseline – they're just more solid than their opponents – and there's no sense in trying to change their game. You shouldn't try to be inventive just for the sake of it: 'If you play like Rafa Nadal or Novak Djokovic on the baseline, you don't need to surprise anyone. So they just show their top level when they need it. I am a player who plays with a lot of variety all the time, and that's because I need to do that to win matches.'

This is a good style of play for those who aren't so fit: 'I don't play like other players because I am not as strong or as physically fit as they are, so I have to play a different way.'

Belinda Bencic, who was 17 years old when she played in her first grand slam quarter-final, at the 2014 US Open, on 'HOW TO THROW YOUR OPPONENT'S RHYTHM OFF WITH A CHANGE OF PACE' ...

Suddenly change the pace in the rally – take some speed off the ball and give your opponent a different ball to deal with: 'You can't let your opponent settle down to always hitting the same shot. If you can, you should always have them thinking about what is coming next. You can do that by making them move around the court, but you can also do it by changing the pace of your shots, by following several balls hit with lots of power with one that is slower and softer.'

By being unpredictable, you will be putting pressure on your opponent to do something with the ball: 'When she has a slower ball to respond to, she won't be entirely sure what to do, and she may feel under more pressure to win the point.'

But be careful – don't mix it up so much that you end up unsettling yourself: 'The worst thing you can do is use too much variety. If you do that, you might throw yourself off your own rhythm.'

Agnieszka Radwanska, a former Wimbledon finalist, on 'HOW TO MIX IT UP' ...

Don't just hit the same shots on the practice court – take the opportunity to experiment: 'For me, it's always been very important to learn a lot of different shots in practice.'

Do your homework – understand what will make your opponent uncomfortable: 'Studying your opponent allows you to play smart, high-percentage tennis. If you understand court positioning and where the ball is going to come from, you will be able to anticipate your opponent's shots before they are hit. This is a very effective skill to master. For example, I often like to use the drop shot as it catches my opponent off-guard and forces them to come to the net, and then you have drawn them out of position.'

> 'Studying your opponent allows you to play smart tennis.'
> AGNIESZKA RADWANSKA

Greg Rusedski, a former US Open finalist, on 'HOW TO MAKE THE MOST OF BEING LEFT-HANDED' ...

Lefties supposedly use a different part of their brains, and that's why they look at tennis differently. Embrace the fact that only ten per cent of people are left-handed: 'Embrace being different.'

Swing a serve out wide: 'The serve is a big advantage when you are playing a right-handed opponent. On the ad court, you can hit a swinging serve that goes out wide, which goes into their backhand, and they will probably have a double-handed backhand, so that will open up the court. On the deuce court, a good tactic is a kick serve out wide, as they will be used to the ball spinning the other way, so that's a massive advantage. The biggest points in tennis tend to be started on the ad court – breakpoints and game-points are usually on that side – so the lefty has a big weapon on that side of using that swinging serve out wide. If you're serving to another lefty, a serve out wide on the ad court will play into their forehand and their strength, so you have to rethink your approach.'

Everything in this world is made for right-handed people, and that means that left-handed people are more susceptible to injuries. But do what you can to adjust, such as putting your racket grip on the 'wrong' way: 'Most racket grips are put on for right-handed players, but do them the opposite way as then the racket will feel a lot more comfortable in your hand.'

Attack a right-hander's backhand: 'The right-hander cannot just follow the normal patterns of play against a left-hander, as they have to think about things in a different way, with the ball coming from a different direction. Against a left-hander, a right-hander can't just play on auto-pilot.'

> **'Do your racket grip in the opposite way to a right-hander.'**
> GREG RUSEDSKI

Mats Wilander, a former world No. 1,
on 'HOW TO BEAT A LEFT-HANDED OPPONENT' ...

Do to them what they're going to do to you – they're going to be bringing you out wide with a slice serve, and you should be doing the same: 'For a right-handed player, the easiest serve to hit is a slice serve, but that's also the worst serve to hit against a right-handed opponent as that's right into their forehand. But when you've got a left-handed opponent, that's the play – you have to slice the ball into their backhand as much as possible.'

If it's a long time since you played against a left-handed opponent, prepare by finding another lefty to serve at you on the practice court: 'It takes time to get used to a lefty's serve. And you want to be used to it before the match starts.'

Don't get caught up in thinking that you always have to attack their backhand: 'I've made that mistake so many times. If you do that, you're not playing your game. You're playing the guy, and only the guy. You're thinking too much about your opponent, and that can make you tentative, and you can stop hitting through the ball.'

Jiri Vesely, who is 6ft 6in,
on 'HOW TO MAKE THE MOST OF YOUR HEIGHT' ...

If you're taller, you're definitely going to have more chance at the net than if you're a small guy. But don't do anything that's going to make yourself uncomfortable: 'Everyone has their own style, and so you shouldn't go to the net on every ball if you don't like doing that. If you're better from the baseline, then stay on the baseline.'

As a tall player, it's even more important to work on your movement. You should be working on that every day: 'If you have the shots of a big guy – including a big serve – but you can move like a small guy then you are going to be a great player.'

It would be a waste of your height not to have a great serve: 'When you serve well, you're going to get some free points, or you're going to have a great chance to attack with the second ball.'

Sara Errani, the 2012 French Open finalist, who is 5ft 4in,
on 'HOW TO BEAT TALLER, MORE POWERFUL OPPONENTS' ...

Make sure that the match doesn't become a power contest, as you will lose that. Play your opponent on your terms, not on theirs: 'You have to target their weaknesses. OK, so you're not as powerful as they are, but maybe you have better movement, or court positioning, or you are better at producing angles or putting spin on the ball. You do whatever you can to play points the way that suits your game and not theirs. If they don't like running, you need to get them to run. Slow it down. Mix it up. Give them different angles and spins to think about. Do what you can to make them uncomfortable.'

Don't be intimidated: 'There are going to be occasions when your opponent simply hits the ball with so much power that you don't have much time to react in the way you want. But that doesn't mean you should fear them. Remember that you have other strengths, which your opponent doesn't. As a junior, I sometimes used to worry that I wouldn't be able to beat the taller girls, but I soon realised that I could.'

Do your homework: 'It's important to know an opponent's game and to think beforehand about how you are going to beat them. I like to sit down with my coach before a match and talk through strategies.'

Get in shape: 'While you might not be able to outhit an opponent, you need to have great fitness, so, if needed, you can run down and retrieve as many balls as possible. It helps to be quick around the court, as that gives you a strength, a weapon, to use against them.'

Don't take any extra satisfaction from beating a taller, more powerful opponent: 'You take your satisfaction from winning matches, not from the build of your opponent.'

Jack Sock, who won the 2014 Wimbledon men's doubles title in partnership with **Vasek Pospisil,**
on 'HOW TO COPE WHEN YOU'RE PLAYING INTO THE SUN'...

Adjust your position on the baseline so you're not looking directly into the sun when you serve: 'Obviously, you're going to want to wear a hat. But you can also help yourself by moving left or right from your usual serving position so that you don't get blinded when you toss the ball up and then look up. You could also think about making an adjustment to your ball toss, but you don't want to be making too many changes.'

The greatest mistake you can make when looking into the sun is getting frustrated: 'Everyone has their moments when they get blinded by the sun. It's the same for everyone.'

Your opponent is probably going to be lobbing the ball up there to test you on the overhead – that's what you should be doing when you have the sun behind you – but it's OK to let the ball bounce first: 'That's a decision you're going to have to make in the moment. It's whatever you're more comfortable with. Do whatever you think is going to give you the best chance of winning the point.'

Fabio Fognini, who has been ranked in the world's top 20, on 'HOW TO RECOVER FROM A BAD START' ...

Keep believing in yourself: 'You have to tell yourself to keep fighting because if you do that, you're going to give yourself a chance. If you believe in yourself, you can achieve anything you want.'

Don't just keep on playing in the same way – you need to make changes to your game: 'When you've had a bad start to the match, you have to be thinking about ways to improve your game and what you are going to do differently to get yourself out of that situation. It's not going to be something like changing how you hit your forehand or hit your backhand, but something in your mind, and the way you're thinking about the match and your opponent.'

Sometimes, your body will start to feel better as the match continues. So keep going: 'It sometimes happens that your body feels bad at the beginning of the match, but then your body starts to feel better, and your touch on the ball improves, too.'

Relish the fight: 'A comeback is always difficult. Once you come back and you're in that final set, you know you're in a good war.'

Tracy Austin, a former world No. 1, on 'HOW TO PLAY WELL IN THE WIND' ...

Look at the flags and trees: 'Some players can go a set without realising which way the wind is going. If there's a flag or there are trees around, use them to help give you an indication of how the wind is blowing and how it will affect the ball. Against the wind you're going to want to hit the ball a little higher for security and to maintain depth. With the wind, you're going to hit with a little more spin to keep the ball in. If there's a crosswind, aim four feet inside the sidelines so the ball doesn't drift out. If you lob, you may have to hit it harder and higher from one end and then with more spin from the other.'

Make little steps up until the moment you hit the ball: 'The ball is going to move at the last moment so you will need to make adjustments.'

Staying patient will win you matches: 'When I beat Martina Navratilova to win the US Open in 1981, it was a really windy day and my attitude was one of the top three assets I had that day. She was upset by it and I used that. You have to be mentally tough, and have control over your emotions.'

Caroline Garcia, considered by **Andy Murray** to be a future women's world No. 1, on 'HOW TO PLAY IN THE HEAT' ...

Don't radically change your game: 'I wouldn't suggest trying to shorten the points to save energy, as that's always difficult to do, and I think you have to play your game and trust yourself. You have to remember that if it's difficult for you in the heat, it will also be difficult for your opponent. It wouldn't be a good time to totally change your game and to go for too many winners. Just play your game and then you will see.'

Keep out of the sun before you are due on court: 'Try not to spend too much time outside before your match as you don't want to be exposed to the sun too much.'

If you can, put a towel in a freezer and take it out just before you go on court: 'Every time you change ends, put it around your neck.'

If you don't eat properly, you're going to end up feeling dizzy: 'You should eat the same amount when it's very warm as you would do on another day. I would suggest eating around three hours before you go on court, as that will give the food some time to digest. On a hot day, you still need to be moving well, and you don't want the food sitting in your stomach when you're on court. To top up your energy levels, have an energy bar or a banana between games.'

You have to drink lots of water but not too much as that can cause you problems: 'But if you're not sure if you are drinking the right amount of water, it's better to drink too much water than too little. If you have drunk too much, you can always take a toilet break. And remember that it's important to keep on drinking during the match.'

Caroline Garcia on 'HOW TO PLAY ON A COLD DAY' ...

Wrap yourself with towels during changeovers: 'Put them over your legs and your shoulders as you sit down on your chair. And don't sit still – keep your legs moving when you're sitting there. When you get up off that chair, you want your body to be ready for the next point.'

Don't stand still between points – keep moving at all times: 'You don't want your muscles to get cold – it's better to sweat too much than to be freezing.'

Leander Paes, a former doubles world No. 1, on 'HOW TO READ YOUR OPPONENT'S GAME' ...

Look for clues about where your opponent is going to play the ball: 'Vision is a big thing in tennis, especially on the return of serve or on the volley, as you have so little time to react. So a lot of it is anticipation. You have to look at things like where the ball toss goes with the serve. And then when you're looking at the player returning serve, you have a look at their stance, and how open they are, and try to work out where they are going to hit the ball.'

Anticipation comes from experience and repetition. But it also comes from studying your opponents: 'You get to know the idiosyncrasies of each opponent and what shots they like to hit. Before I play a match, I like to check out the last three months of matches, and to look at what they do in every situation. For example, what does he do on a stretch backhand return? As you get deeper into the tournament, everyone's in a good rhythm and one or two shots can make the difference, and the recordings you've watched become more and more important.'

Dominika Cibulkova, a former Australian Open finalist, on 'HOW TO READ YOUR OPPONENT'S SERVE' ...

Pay close attention to your opponent's ball toss, as most players use different tosses for different serves: 'There are a few players who hit different serves with the same toss, and that's not easy to read. But they are rare, so have a good look at the toss. You can usually tell whether your opponent is going to hit a kick serve, or whether they are going to go for a big serve, or whether they are going to go wide, down the "T" or to the body. The sooner you know what they are doing, the more time you have to prepare your own shot.'

Look into their eyes: 'Some players are in the habit of looking where they are about to serve.'

Never take your eyes off the ball: 'You should be concentrating on the ball at all times, from before the ball toss.'

Get some advance information about your opponent's style from your coach (or do some scouting yourself).

If you're playing a left-handed opponent, they have an advantage, so it will probably take you longer to read their serve.

If you're having difficulties reading their serve, there are other ways of causing problems for your opponent: 'Think about changing your own position on the court to return serve, and make sure that you change enough so that your opponent sees and has to think more. For example, if my opponent has hit five aces wide past me, I will stand a little wider, and then maybe jump back a bit.'

Caroline Wozniacki, a former world No. 1,
on 'HOW TO BREAK AN OPPONENT'S SERVE' ...

Try to get a feel for where your opponent likes to serve the most: 'By getting into a rhythm on your returns, you'll put pressure on them from the start.'

Don't become too defensive or over-think the points: 'If you do those things, it can only go wrong.'

It's very important to attack the second serve: 'This is a great opportunity for you to be on top from the start of the point.'

Unsettle your opponent by varying where you stand, moving a metre or two to one side, and then back again: 'However, it's important to keep your focus on the ball, anticipating which side it is going, and taking it early.'

View breakpoints on your opponent's serve as an opportunity rather than something to feel pressured about: 'Remember that it's the server who will feel the most pressure at those moments.'

Ana Konjuh, a former junior world No. 1 who as a 16-year-old made the third round of the women's singles tournament at Wimbledon 2014, on **'HOW TO OVERPOWER YOUR OPPONENT'** ...

Don't hesitate before you play the ball – trust in yourself: 'I've played this way, with a lot of power, since I was a kid, but the most important thing is that you believe in yourself.'

However, the worst thing you can do is to play every shot at 100 per cent power: 'As a kid, I did that a lot, always hitting the ball as hard as I could. But I realised that you can't always play at full power – you also have to use some slice and spin as otherwise you're going to make too many mistakes, with the balls flying over the fence. It's not just about power – you have to make good decisions. If the ball is five metres away from you, and you have to move fast to hit it, you probably want to play a safer shot, and just get the ball back into play. But if the ball is there and there's an opportunity for a winner, go for it.'

Jiri Vesely, who reached the last 32 at a grand slam for the first time at Wimbledon 2014, on **'HOW TO PLAY AGAINST AN INJURED OPPONENT'** ...

Don't make the mistake of playing safe and pushing the ball around. Play harder: 'You don't want to just wait for your opponent's mistakes, as if you're playing safe they're going to think they have a chance. You want them to give up, to retire. Instead of playing safe, you need to be going for your shots, and making everything as difficult as possible for the opponent – you should be showing them that it would be better for them just to give up.'

If your opponent is having trouble with their movement, make them run as much as possible: 'And you also want to make your opponent change direction – that's very effective if they have injured their leg.'

The best advice is to keep focused on your own game: 'Playing against an injured opponent is a very hard situation, especially if you know before the match that there's something wrong with them. When your opponent isn't ready, you have to focus on your own game and just try to play every ball.'

If your opponent starts with an injury, try to break early, maybe even in their first service game: 'Then you're telling your opponent that it's going to be a tough day for them.'

Michael Chang, who hit an underarm serve during his fourth-round match against Ivan Lendl at the 1989 French Open, on 'HOW TO SURPRISE YOUR OPPONENT' ...

(Chang, who was 17 years old, went on to win the tournament.)

Hit an underarm serve: 'It was Andre Agassi who first showed me how effective an underarm serve could be, and how you could unsettle an opponent. He used to do that in junior matches. You had to watch out for that and be on your guard. It was a spur of the moment decision, really, for me to hit an underarm serve during my fourth-round match against Ivan Lendl at the 1989 French Open. I thought to myself, "I could hit a 69mph serve and that would give him something different to deal with." He was forced to come in and he didn't like that. And that underarm serve changed the whole mentality of the match. After that, he became more frustrated that everything wasn't going his way.'

Stand close to the service line to receive a second serve on a big point: 'I did this on match point against Lendl. You have to remember that I was 17 and just out of juniors, and this what we did in the juniors, but it works in men's tennis too. I found that opponents either double-fault, as Lendl did, or they drop the ball short, as they don't want to double-fault on a big point, and then you have a great chance to play a strong return and win the point.'

If you're a baseliner, try serve and volleying every so often, even on big points: 'Your opponent, who doesn't have time to adjust, plays the same ball that he's been playing all day – the ball is floating in the air and you can put it away for a winner.'

Attack the second serve: 'Players don't do this enough. It totally throws your opponent's rhythm off.'

A drop shot can be the most effective shot on clay – you can shake up your opponent: 'You get guys pounding away 10 feet behind the baseline, pounding, pounding, pounding, and they can end it all by suddenly playing a drop shot. The mental side is so important. If you can shake a guy up mentally, if he ends up thinking that he doesn't know what's coming next, and he's no longer sure he can win, that's worth even more to you than one or two winners.'

Mats Wilander, a former world No. 1,
on 'HOW TO PLAY THE BIG POINTS WELL' ...

You have to realise that the big moments aren't just at four-all and deuce: 'A big moment isn't always a big moment for both players; it can just be a big moment for you. Sometimes you can take momentum and carry it without your opponent realising that it was a big moment for you. The best players recognise when it's a big moment and they take their opportunities.'

The more big points you can create early on in the match, the more you will know what to do at four-all and deuce: 'If you're at love-thirty on your opponent's serve, that's a massive point. If you win the next point, you'll have three breakpoints and a really good chance to go a break up. All the big players know what to do at four-all and deuce as they think about what they did to get there. The players who suddenly arrive at a scoreboard big point, and start hitting out, those are the ones who don't make it.'

If you're going to get nervous at four-all and deuce – and most players do get tight on the big points – you had better create a situation where you get nervous at one-all and deuce: 'That will teach you to play when you're tight.'

You need to care about tactics early on in the match: 'Then when it comes to the big points later, you'll know what to do.'

Maria Kirilenko, who has been ranked in the world's top 10,
on 'HOW TO PLAY A TIEBREAK' ...

Winning a tiebreak is all about getting the balance of risk right: 'You have to take risks if you're going to win more tiebreaks than you lose. So if you're returning well, you go for it a bit more, and the same on your serve. That's especially true as you go deeper into a tiebreak, when perhaps people want to play safe rather than taking risks. But, of course, you don't want to be reckless and make lots of mistakes, especially at the beginning of a tiebreak.'

Mistakes are not going to help you, but the worst thing you can do in a tiebreak is to hit a double-fault: 'You have to make your opponent win a point – don't just hand it to them.'

It's often mental strength that decides who wins a tiebreak, not who is stronger physically, or who has the best shots: 'That means concentrating.'

If you win the first set on a tiebreak, don't relax: 'It happens a lot that a player wins the first set in a tiebreak, and then loses the second set, and then suddenly they're having to play a third set. I think it's probably because the player thinks after the tiebreak, "Phew, that was tough, but I did it", and they think the match is almost over, but it's not. You have to keep working in the second set. Your opponent is probably going to be thinking that they have nothing to lose, so they're going to be playing loose.'

Kyle Edmund, who won two junior grand slam doubles titles,
on 'HOW TO PLAY A FINAL SET' ...

If you have just levelled the match to take it into a decider, keep on playing in the same way, as you'll have good momentum: 'The worst thing you can do at that moment is to leave the court for a loo break. If you're desperate, you've got to go, but by leaving the court, you're going to lose some of the momentum. However, if your opponent has just won a set, it would be a good idea to slow down play, and to disrupt the rhythm of the match. Also, if your opponent has just levelled the match, think about what you did well to win the first set and put those thoughts into what you're doing on the court.'

Play with lots of energy at the start of the set: 'If you can get on top of your opponent early in the set, quite often his head will drop and mentally he will go away.'

Take care of your service games because it's important to keep holding your serve to mount pressure on your opponent.

If you are in the lead, don't think about winning the match: 'Stay in the present and focus on one point at a time.'

Ana Konjuh who won junior titles at the Australian Open and US Open,
on 'HOW TO PLAY A FINAL SET' ...

Concentrate on yourself: 'You have to focus on yourself, and what you want to do with the ball. You have to play your game. Playing a final set is very different to playing a first set – by then you've warmed up, you've got the adrenaline, and you're into the match. But you need to make sure that you don't get too caught up in the moment, and that you don't forget what you want to do with the ball.'

If it's your opponent who has just levelled the match, by taking the second set of a best-of-three-set match, take encouragement from how you won the opening set: 'If I've won the first set, and then my opponent levels the match by winning the second set, I'm going to be a bit down. So I need to get myself up. That's a mental process. Physically, I like to get my legs moving at the start of the final set – that often helps me to get back to the level I had reached in the first set.'

Judy Murray, Andy and Jamie's mother and first coach,
on 'HOW TO CLOSE OUT MATCHES' ...

If you feeling anxious when you're in a winning position, you need to think about what's causing that anxiety. It's good to talk about that anxiety, maybe to a coach, a parent or a friend: 'The answers are within you. It's the same with anything – you just need to talk about it, and then you'll find a solution.'

Combat the fear of failure. Instead, have a clear idea in your head about how you have reached that winning position, and about what you want to make happen on the next point: 'Instead of fearing what might happen, think about what you want to make happen on the next point.'

Work hard on the practice court or in the gym – that will give you belief in yourself: 'You have to know that you've done it a million times in practice before. Ultimately, though, you can only improve the way you close your matches by actually playing matches.'

Victoria Azarenka, a multiple grand slam champion,
on 'How to serve out a match' ...

Find the emotional level which allows you to perform at your best: 'Serving for the match is different from other service games, so the emotional level is going to be different. With experience, you will come to know the level that allows you to perform at your best, and also how you control your mental state to reach that level.'

If there is a change of ends before you serve for the match, use those 90 seconds wisely: 'Sometimes as I wait on the chair before trying to serve out a match, I don't think at all. Other times, I will think about a movie I've just watched. Other times, maybe I'll remind myself of what I need to do during the service game, or I'll be trying to get myself pumped up, or, if I'm getting too excited, I'll be telling myself to calm down.'

Stay disciplined – of course, you want to finish in style, with an ace or a big winner, but it would be a mistake to become to obsessed with doing that: 'It depends on the situation. If you're 6-0, 5-0 up, you might as well try. But I always value every point, and you can't ever underestimate your opponent, especially when you're playing at a high level. One moment can change a whole match. I've seen that happen to other players, it's happened for me, and it's happened against me. So it's really important to stay disciplined. That's what takes you to a high level, and you want to stay there.'

Sloane Stephens, a semi-finalist at the 2013 Australian Open,
on 'HOW TO PLAY MATCH POINTS' ...

Don't play the point any differently to the ones that came before it: 'You've worked all the points prior to that to get to match point, so stick with the same strategy that has got you that far, and don't suddenly do something different. Stay aggressive if you can. One of the reasons some players are better than others at playing match points is that they keep on going for shots after they get ahead.'

The same advice applies if your opponent has a match point: 'Keep playing as you have been all match, and don't change that strategy.'

If you're feeling tense or nervous, take a couple of deep breaths and jump around a bit.

If you are serving, the biggest mistake you can make is to hit a double-fault: 'So make your first serve.'

John Isner, who won an 11-hour match against Nicolas Mahut at the 2010 Wimbledon Championships, on 'HOW TO WIN AN EPIC' ...

Avoid great emotional highs and lows – you want to stay at a nice, steady, solid level: 'I know that if I can stay calm, I'm going to be very tough to beat.'

As well as taking a physical toll, a long match takes a mental toll. But you mustn't let up: 'You can't really train for the marathon matches. You work hard all year, and try to get in the best possible shape, but if you get involved in a long match, have faith in your fitness and try to compete as best as you can.'

Take some pleasure: 'When you're playing in close matches, it's the best – that's why I play.'

During the changes of ends, you're taking a physical break, but you shouldn't be taking a mental break: 'I'll be nibbling on an energy bar. I'll also try to keep a lot of salt in my body – I've had cramp before in the past, so I put salt in my drinks. But don't take a mental break. There have been times when I've gone walkabout on the court and it doesn't bode well for me, or for anybody.'

Think about ways to keep the points short: 'You're not going to be so fresh in the final set, so I try to conserve energy when I can.'

PLAYING DOUBLES

MEN'S AND WOMEN'S DOUBLES

Bob and Mike Bryan, the most successful doubles team in tennis history, on 'HOW TO BEHAVE TOWARDS YOUR DOUBLES PARTNER' ...

Always be positive when speaking to your partner on the court: 'Sometimes you're going to have to fake it. You're only half of the team, and you need your partner feeling great and playing the best that he can.'

Never order your partner around. Never roll your eyes when talking to your partner. If you've just had a bad defeat, clear the air right away. And be honest: 'We like to hash it out pretty quickly after a match. We will tell it straight. Two professionals who aren't brothers would probably never say the stuff that we say. We get it out there, even if it's not friendly. We'll say some really personal stuff that we know will cut the other twin to the core. But that means that we can let off a lot of steam, and clear the air. Other players might have some lingering problems and drama that will get them in trouble for a whole month or two months and could end the partnership. Obviously it helps that we're twins and we have a bond which is never going to break. We're not looking around for another partner, and the other one knows that.'

Violence should never be condoned – but sometimes it can work: 'We've got physical. We've thrown punches and thrown stuff. We've broken guitars against the wall, thrown shoes, and hurled a glass bottle of pills across the room, shattering it. Our biggest fight was after a first-round match at Wimbledon one year. We had had a barn-burner on the court. We actually won, but it was a terrible match. We threw some punches in the back of the car that was taking us from Wimbledon, and then when we got to the apartment, we ran up the stairs and broke some stuff, including a guitar. We were so pissed off with each other. And then we ended up winning the tournament. There have been other times that we've been on a flight, jabbing at each other, and a stewardess has come up to us and said, "Is everything OK here?" We will wait until she leaves and then go back at it.'

Roy Emerson, a winner of 16 grand slam doubles titles,
on 'HOW TO PLAY BRILLIANT DOUBLES' ...

Your first job is always to protect your partner: 'Don't play a shot that's going to get your partner killed. Too often you see two people playing doubles and it doesn't look as though they are playing together as a team. This isn't singles; it's doubles. You have to look out for your partner at all times.'

You should know where your partner is at all times – without looking back.

Don't go for too much with the return of serve: 'You don't have to go for winners the whole time. It's especially important that the player on the forehand side isn't erratic and doesn't make too many unforced errors, as otherwise his partner on the backhand side is always going to find himself facing fifteen-love. If one of you is more erratic, a bit more of a shot-maker, he should play on the backhand side as he's the guy who is going to get more of the breakpoint opportunities, so it makes more sense to take a bit more risk with the return of serve.'

Take some pace off your serve to get a first-serve percentage of around 85 per cent: 'You don't need a big serve to win doubles matches. It's best to take some of the pace off the ball and to land your first serve. If you get your first-serve percentage up to 80 or 85 per cent, you're going to make it extremely difficult for your opponents to break you. But if you start hitting a lot of second serves, you're going to be in trouble as a good doubles team can win 80 per cent of second serves they face.'

If you're going to serve and volley, get as close to the net as possible for that first volley, so you don't have to play the ball off your shoelaces.

Choose your partner carefully: 'Picking the right doubles partner is so important. If you can't converse, and can't communicate to each other what you're trying to achieve, you're not going to get very far.'

Mahesh Bhupathi, a former doubles world No. 1, who won 12 grand slam doubles titles, on 'HOW TO CHOOSE A DOUBLES PARTNER' ...

Find someone who will complement your strengths and weaknesses: 'Some players have a lot of agility, and some have power, some serve and volley better, and some return better. It's always good to have two partners who have the mix of all those strengths if you want to have a good team. If you have a good serve, you should be looking for someone who can knock off the volleys. If you have a good return, then a partner who is intimidating at the net would enhance that return. If you're weak from the baseline, you need someone who is very solid from the back of the court, so you can make up for that weakness.'

However, it can work well having a team of two players with very similar styles: 'You can have a team strength.'

Jonny Marray, who won the men's doubles competition at Wimbledon in 2012 with Frederik Nielsen, on **'THE BEST KIND OF DOUBLES PARTNER'** ...

Pick a friend: 'You're going to be spending a lot of time together – you've got to enjoy their company. The worst thing is playing with someone who doesn't let me stay relaxed so that I can enjoy playing. You get enough pressure from yourself and your opponents, so the last thing you need is your partner putting pressure on you too. I've got to be able to trust my partner to be in my corner all the time.'

David Macpherson is the most successful doubles coach in tennis history – he has worked with the **Bryan brothers**, and was a consultant to Switzerland's winning Davis Cup team at the 2014 final, which saw **Roger Federer** and **Stan Wawrinka** combine to take the doubles rubber. Here are his tips on **'HOW TO HAVE SUCCESS AS A DOUBLES TEAM'** ...

You need to find a way of constantly pushing each other: 'At the same time, you need to stay positive with each other and to maintain team chemistry. That's easier said than done.'

Never ease off on the practice court: 'Practise at 100 per cent intensity every session and never let that slip.'

Don't play the blame game after defeats: 'If both players look at themselves first, rather than at their partner, it will promote accountability.'

Bob and Mike Bryan, the first doubles team to win more than 100 titles, on **'HOW TO GET IN SHAPE FOR DOUBLES'** ...

You shouldn't train for doubles in the same way you train for singles: 'We work as hard as singles players; it's just that we're doing different stuff. We're in the gym as much as we're on the court. As a singles player, you need to do a lot of cardio to be ready to play. You don't need that as much in doubles. In doubles, the points are much shorter. You need a strong core and strong legs. But our legs are pretty skinny compared to the singles players.'

Doubles is a fast-twitch game. So you need to be able to make quick, explosive movements: 'As a singles player on the tour these days, you can play a pretty smooth game. Sometimes it's easier on the body playing singles than doubles. Obviously playing singles is more gruesome on the body with the endurance, but in doubles you're always crouched down and you have to make very explosive moves. When the singles guys come and play doubles, they tend to be a little flat-footed. It takes their eye a little while to get adjusted. You have to see everything way out in front. You have to be fast.'

You should be doing lots of preventative work, and with every part of your body: 'For a tennis player, your body is your business, so if we have a week off between tournaments, we're in the gym a couple of hours a day.'

Do a lot of resistance band sprints and movement: 'You put the harness on, and move about the court – back-pedalling, changing direction, that sort of stuff. We also do that in sand, which strengthens your ankles. So, when you get back on the court, it feels a little easier. We're always in that crouch position, and you want to get out of that position as quickly as possible so we do a lot of static stuff and biometric jumps.'

Ross Hutchins, who has been ranked in the world's top 30, on 'HOW TO WARM UP FOR DOUBLES' ...

You need to warm up for twice as long before a doubles match as you would do before playing singles: 'A singles player can work his way into a match. In doubles, you have to be sharp from the first point. In doubles, because it's so serve-dominated and because of the sudden-death format on the tour, you can't have a slow start.'

Warm up together – spend an hour on the practice court with your doubles partner.

Hit from the back of the court for 20 minutes, starting with shots down the middle and then moving on to cross-court strokes.

You need 20 minutes to warm up your volleys: 'One of you comes to the net, with the other staying at the back. The volleyer would practise forehand volleys cross-court, forehand volleys down the line, and then switch over to the backhand. And then we practise our first volley. The player doing that starts just outside the baseline, and then comes in to hit a first forehand volley cross-court. So the other player is then practising their second shot. And then you switch over to do the same with the backhand. I would suggest doing around four each of the different first volleys, so you're hitting around 16 each. And then switch over.'

Spend 20 minutes on your serves and playing some points: 'It's all about getting yourself match sharp.'

After leaving the practice court, have some food, a shower and rest.

Twenty minutes before you're due on court, go to the gym or somewhere you can make quick, sharp movements: 'Do some squat jumps so you're going to be ready on the court to make explosive movements. Being explosive generally means that your mind is switched on. As you walk out, you're ready to go. You're thinking, "I'm not going to miss easy shots, I'm not going to be lethargic, I'm going to put pressure on our opponents." If you're switched on physically after waking up your body, you're going to be switched on mentally and you won't make any silly errors. Two bad points can cost you a set in doubles.'

Bob and Mike Bryan
on 'HOW TO AVOID BASIC ERRORS IN DOUBLES' ...

If you're going to serve wide, make sure you tell your net-man: 'If you don't tell him, and he's close to the middle of the court, you're going to get burned down the line the whole time. That's a common mistake.'

Don't be passive at the net: 'You mustn't be slow and fearful.'

You shouldn't be on your heels: 'Your weight should always be going forwards, and you should be hitting the ball in front of you. You need to be on your toes.'

Ross Hutchins
on 'HOW TO GET YOUR DOUBLES FORMATION RIGHT' ...

The important thing is to play to your strengths: 'If you don't like coming to the net, or if you don't like hitting backhands, or if you want to avoid a shot which you think will let you down in certain situations, it's quite easy in doubles to cover that.'

When you're serving, it's easy to cover your weakness: 'As the server, you're in charge of the game. For example, if you're trying to cover your backhand, you would serve and then immediately move to your right to go to your forehand. So if you're serving to the ad court, your partner is in the left service box. You serve and then take two steps to the right and that puts you in prime position to take on your opponent and hold your serve. You're suddenly in a position of strength, in the forehand corner. You're more comfortable, and your opponents are probably going to be a little bit confused.'

Keep the instructions simple. You want to confuse your opponents, not your partner: 'When I'm serving, I tell my partner where I'm going to serve and where I want him to go. And that's it.'

Don't listen to the traditionalists who say you have to be at the net. If you don't feel comfortable hitting volleys, stay back: 'In amateur tennis you see so many people missing volleys and missing smashes, and I'm sure they're thinking to themselves, "I don't want to be there." Well, you don't have to be there. If you want to play two at the back, then play two at the back. That's saying to your opponents, "We feel like our back court game is better than your all-round game and that's why we're choosing to stay at the back of the court – we're confident that we're better than you guys." Let them come in and just trust your groundstrokes.'

Sometimes both players start at the back and come to the net together: 'You stay back until the right opportunity and then you go in together. This way, amateurs can avoid most tricky volleys. I would highly recommend playing two at the back on return. It can be quite imposing for your opponents when you're both at the back and then you come in together. It's like a wave hitting your opponent. They will feel under pressure to play a good shot, and they'll often make an error.'

If one player in the team is very comfortable hitting volleys, you have to use them at the net as much as possible: 'If they're serving, they should serve and volley, and if they're returning, they should hit and come in. That's quite basic. If you're at the net already – your partner is serving or receiving – you have to look to get involved. That means taking risks and moving to the middle. You're trying to take over the court; you're trying to finish off the point quickly. You're trying to get in the eyeline of your opponent. You're faking, you're moving, you're making bold moves to plant seeds in people's heads about what is going to happen on the next point. That causes confusion, tension, worry.'

Generally, if you're good at the net, stand as close as possible: 'In amateur tennis, everyone always stands too far back. I always encourage players, especially when they are dominating the rally, or if their partner is at the back of the court to cover the lob, to get in close. You should be one or two feet away. You're imposing at the net. You feel part of the point. The angles are reduced. Therefore you can take more balls and get more involved.'

Confuse your opponents with the Australian or 'I' formation: 'The server stands close to the middle of the court, as you need to be able to cover going both ways. So the returner doesn't know which way you're going to go. Your partner crouches down, around a foot to the side of where you're going to serve. So if you're serving to the deuce court, your partner will crouch about a foot into the ad court. And if you're serving to the ad court, your partner will be a foot into the deuce court. The returner won't know where you're going to go.'

> **'Amateurs always stand too far back.'**
> ROSS HUTCHINS

Use the Australian formation to target an opponent's weakness: 'Maybe your opponent can only hit the forehand cross-court – that happens at the top of the game, too. It's easier for your partner to cover certain areas when they're standing in a neutral position in the middle of the court. Whereas if they are standing in a regular position and want to cover the forehand cross-court, it's further to run, and there's more chance that your opponent will hit a winner past you.'

Crossing is important when you're using a normal doubles formation, with one at the back and the partner on the other side at the net: 'If you want to have success, you need to call crosses. So you agree, say, that after the serve goes in, you're going to switch. That causes confusion and uncertainty on the other side of the net. The net player can be really close to the net, and as he moves across the court, he just has to touch the ball in the direction of your opponent at the net and it's going to be a winner. That's because your opponent is going to have such little time to react. You can also make crosses when you're returning, but again that has to be agreed in advance.'

Create even more uncertainty on the other side of the net by changing formations: 'Maybe consider doing one third of points with a regular formation, one third "I" formation and one third crossing.'

Vasek Pospisil, who won the 2014 Wimbledon title when playing his first tournament with **Jack Sock,** on 'HOW TO MAKE A GOOD START TO A NEW DOUBLES PARTNERSHIP'...

You need to be comfortable discussing each other's weaknesses: 'It's great if the personalities match and you get on well with your partner, but you also need to be comfortable talking about your strengths and weaknesses as individuals and as a team. You can then make game plans aimed to use your strengths to expose your opponents' weaknesses.'

But it's really important to stay positive and to keep any criticism out of the picture: 'The biggest mistake a team can make is to start getting negative with one another. As soon as that happens, it's trouble, and it will all be downhill from there.'

Peng Shuai, who has held the doubles world No. 1 ranking, on 'HOW TO HAVE A GOOD RELATIONSHIP WITH YOUR DOUBLES PARTNER' ...

Go shopping, go out for dinner, have some fun together off the court: 'If you can enjoy each other's company away from the court, I think it's much more likely that you will play good tennis together during matches. If you're friends, there's going to be less pressure on court, as you're both going to be more likely to just have fun with it. You will be more comfortable with each other.'

Recognise that your partner can't play well every match: 'You have to be understanding and not get angry. There are going to be just as many days when you're not playing so well. Some days, you will fight, but try to make up as soon as you can.'

Jonas Bjorkman, who achieved the career grand slam in doubles, on 'HOW TO ENCOURAGE YOUR PARTNER' ...

Don't say 'he', say 'we': 'Sometimes you hear guys saying, "Yeah, he lost his serve at 5-4," and for me I can never understand how you can say that "he" lost his serve. It's always a team effort. You can have a great serve but if you don't have a guy who helps you at the net, you're not going to hold serve.'

Ross Hutchins, who has been ranked in the world's top 30, on 'HOW TO SPEAK TO YOUR DOUBLES PARTNER AFTER A BAD DEFEAT' ...

Don't make any jokes: 'Even if you get on well, don't joke around. Don't make a jokey comment like, "Gosh, that was a bad result." It should be more like, "We really struggled out there today."'

Be open and honest about what happened on the court. If you played badly, then say so. But while it's good to admit your faults, you should never apologise: 'Some people struggle with this. You can't play well every day. I think it's important to acknowledge that it's a bad loss, or to acknowledge how well your opponents played. However, don't say sorry as that's going to put even more of a dampener on things. You can't do any more than try your hardest.'

Never tell your partner that he should say sorry for a poor performance: 'Don't start pointing out your partner's failings. If it's someone you play with regularly, I would think that he would openly admit to playing badly. And you shouldn't have to tell them because they should know themselves. If they don't say it, deep down you know it and he knows it too. And that's when you can get tension in a partnership, when someone isn't open. When someone thinks they're better and that their partner is regularly messing up, that's when most partnerships break up, as people are always thinking that they could do better with someone else. Over the course of the year, you will probably have as many bad days as your partner. It evens out.'

> **'Don't start pointing out your partner's failings.'**
> ROSS HUTCHINS

Don't bad-mouth your partner behind his back. If you've got something to say, say it to your partner, not to others: 'You will hear players criticising their partners to other people, but they never actually speak to each other about what the problem is. That leads to partnerships splitting up.'

Immediately start talking to your partner about the next time you will play together, and what you have to work on before then: 'That will stop you thinking negatively about your partner.'

Jamie Murray, winner of the mixed doubles with **Jelena Jankovic**
at the Wimbledon Championships in 2007,
on **'HOW TO COMMUNICATE WITH YOUR DOUBLES PARTNER'** ...

Hold some tennis balls up to your mouth when you're telling your partner
where you're going to serve. That way, your opponents can't lip-read:
'Players are always looking at their opponents' mouths to get an inkling
about where the ball is going.'

Make sure you tell your partner where you're going to
serve or return: 'If your partner knows where
the ball is going, he or she's going to be much
more effective, as they'll be better placed to
anticipate what's going to happen next. It's
even more important now that guys are
hitting harder, so the reaction time is
much shorter.'

The friendlier you are off the court,
the easier it is to communicate on
the court: 'If I'm playing with
someone I know well, I
wouldn't hesitate to say, "Look,
stop doing this. Or try this." And I don't think
they would mind me saying that. But if I pitch up
to play with Joe Bloggs for the week, and start
telling him what to do, he or she's going to be
thinking, "Just shut up".'

Be willing to take criticism: 'If I'm doing
something wrong or if I should be doing
something better, I want to hear about it because that's going to help the
team to be successful. I wouldn't want my partner to stay quiet – it's much
better to be open.'

Don't talk all the way through the changeover: 'It can be nice just to sit
there in silence, as it's a timeout from the match. It can be good to just sit
down and think about the match rather than talking about it. But if you've
got something that needs saying, then say it.'

Give off good energy: 'If you're just moping, that's not going to inspire
your partner. If your partner misses a shot, don't drop your head.'

Bob and Mike Bryan, who are the first doubles team to win more than 100 titles, on 'HOW TO HOLD SERVE' ...

You need a higher first-serve percentage in doubles than you do in singles: 'In singles you can serve 50 per cent and be fine, but in doubles you need to serve high 70s. So a lot of the time we won't go for the flat bomb. We will take off 10mph. We'll go for the higher-percentage serve.'

The body serve is great in doubles: 'It cuts down their angles and jams them and their options up, and that frees up your partner at the net to poach. Also, when you go for a body serve, you're not going to miss the serve wide so that helps to keep your percentage up.'

Have a plan for every point: 'We make a quick signal before the point. It really helps the guy at the net to know where his partner is going to serve, as then you have a beat on the return. For example, if your partner is going to serve wide, you need to be covering the line. A lot of the time it's just one word here or there; we don't need a 15-second conversation. We keep it short, with code words. The server is usually the one who decides where the ball is going to go – he's the one who is calling the pitches. Unless the poacher really sees a tendency or feels strongly about a particular serve. The rest of the time, it's the server who calls the shots.'

If you're playing a really hot returner, think about changing your formation: 'We try to create indecision in the other team's heads.'

You don't want any surprises – do your homework: 'When we walk on court, we want to already know where they like to return. Do what you can to take away their best shots.'

Bob and Mike Bryan on 'HOW TO BREAK SERVE' ...

You have to hit an aggressive return: 'In doubles, it's not just about making the return. You have to go for it. When one of us hits a great return, and it's a laser-beam, and it just misses, the other one will say, "That was positive, that was a great way to hit it." We like to praise those misses because we know that, over time, you will get rewarded for taking that sort of risk.'

If you hit a singles return on a doubles court, it's going to get smashed: 'Singles and doubles are completely different games. The best singles players can't just walk on to a doubles court and play good matches. It's something you have to work on. You have to hit it near the alley and low. Otherwise it's a throwaway return.'

The player at the net has to be really active and aggressive with the poaching: 'You want to make strong diagonal moves to cut off shots, and make it hard for your opponents with the first volley, and try to create some doubt and indecision in their minds. If you can make a good return, and then a good poach, you will be in great shape to break serve.'

Do your research on your opponents' serving tendencies and where they serve on the big points: 'That will help you to be really aggressive.'

Daniel Nestor, a multiple doubles grand slam champion, on 'HOW TO RETURN SERVE IN DOUBLES' ...

Don't just play safe and block – take a proper swing at the ball: 'People used to say that you should block the ball back on your return, especially when facing fast first serves, with the aim to keep the ball as low as possible. But that was what was happening in the 1990s. The game has changed now, with the advances in racket and string technology, and also with the different balls. If you're facing a fast server and feel rushed on your return, maybe take a step back.'

Ignore the guy at net who will be moving about and trying to put you off: 'It's his job to distract you, but it's your job to ignore him.'

Don't forget that if you hit the ball hard and clean, your opponent will find it very difficult to get it back, even if you hit the ball straight at him, or if he moves across to intercept.

Go cross-court most of the time: 'Some teams like to cross, so a good play against them is to return the ball down the line more often than you would normally. But against most teams, your staple shot will be cross-court.'

Vary your returns by playing a lob every now and then.

Daniel Nestor on 'HOW TO DOMINATE THE SERVICE BOX' ...

Make an aggressive start to the match by hitting some winners: 'That's going to have your opponents thinking, "Oh boy, he's all over the net, and we're going to have to play the perfect return or shot to get past this guy." A good start can set the tone for the match.'

React to the ball – rather than trying to anticipate what's going to happen: 'I see some players always trying to work out in their heads what's going to happen next, but I think it's often best just to watch the ball and play the shot. If you're over-aggressive with your anticipation, then you're going to take yourself out of the play and that's going to make you and your partner vulnerable.'

Move about the net to distract the returner: 'You want him to be thinking about what you're doing rather than the shot he's about to play.'

Move forwards, and don't turn your shoulder too much: 'You want to get as close to the net as possible, to close off the angles. It's best to move forward first, rather than turning sideways. This relates to the point about reacting to the ball and not trying to guess what's going to happen. Turn your shoulders too early, guess wrong, and you've taken yourself out of the play.'

Max Mirnyi, a former world No. 1 doubles player, on 'HOW TO AVOID BEING PASSED OR LOBBED AT THE NET' ...

The way tennis is played today, you need something special to come into the net on: 'Hitting deep down the middle of the court is often a good approach against a counter-puncher, someone who loves seeing a target. Think about the geometry – the angles just won't be as appealing for your opponent when they are hitting from the "T" rather than around the doubles alley. Another option is a mid-court slice where you force the opposition to come forward and to shorten up the backswing on their stroke – they will often misfire with the passing shot or hit the ball up to give you a put-away volley.'

> 'Impose yourself at the net.'
> MAX MIRNYI

The closer you stand to the net, the less of an angle your opponents have for a passing shot: 'However, make sure you're not leaving too much court open to be lobbed. If you don't win the point with the first volley, you must establish yourself at the net. A player should be ready to move more quickly against a down-the-line passing shot rather than the cross-court shot, as an instinctive volleyer always feels as though he or she has an extra split-second to cover the cross-court shot. That's because the ball has to travel slightly longer coming across the court than down the line. Remember that tennis is a game of angles – it's usually the players who make best use of the full width of the court who win.'

Constantly monitor the external factors, such as sun, wind and new balls: 'That will help you think about the options available to your opponent for the passing shot.'

Make the most of any physical advantage you have to make your opponent feel uncomfortable: 'Impose yourself at net, by putting balls away, especially those that are above the net. This will help you to feel more confident, and at the same time send discomforting messages to your opponents.'

Study your opponents' tendencies for passing shots, and which shot they like to play and when: 'Try to find some video footage, and speak to other players who have played against them recently. And then when the match starts, be sharp and alert from the first point, and try memorising everything that your opponents do. In between points and during changeovers, remind yourself of those patterns. And then, when it comes to the crucial point of the match, you are more likely to find yourself in the right place on the court to play the winning shots.'

Don't get ahead of yourself: 'Many players at all levels of the game get ahead of themselves constructing a point rather than hitting a ball that is coming towards them right then. It is important to be focused on the job in hand. There is no point planning your position at the net if your approach shot does not have enough conviction or accuracy.'

At the same time, keep in mind that there is an exception to every rule: 'Stay in the moment and play the ball, even if you're not in a perfect position.'

Bob and Mike Bryan on 'HOW TO POACH AT THE NET' ...

The key to a good poach is being close to the net – it's about exploiting the middle of the court: 'In doubles, poaching will always be relevant. Even when you watch all the guys who rip from the baseline, their net play is still pretty accurate, moving towards the middle. The key to doubles is getting across the middle and exploiting the middle of the court.'

Keep your hands way out in front of the body. A good split step is huge. You need a quick burst of energy: 'A lot of times it's about moving toward the net strap and getting as close to the net as possible, that's what makes for a put-away volley and an easy intercept. It's about closing the net down.'

Throw in a head fake, play a game with your opponents.

Wait for as long as possible before making your move – until your opponent is committed to their shot: 'You don't want to move too early, and you don't want to move too late. You want to make that move right, as they've committed to their shot. But when you do move, you have to move quickly.'

Visualise where you think the ball's going to be, and then react to that, go and get that space on the court: 'It's too late if you're still thinking.'

When you move, move forward in a diagonal direction: 'You don't want to move too laterally, but remember to make it quick.'

You need your partner to be making a lot of low returns: 'If they can keep the ball low, your opponents will have to hit up, and you're going to have more opportunities.'

Jonny Marray, a former Wimbledon doubles champion, on 'HOW TO MAKE THE FIRST VOLLEY COUNT IN DOUBLES' ...

Be decisive – you can't allow yourself to be in two minds when you hit the ball: 'If there's any hesitation in your mind about what you're going to do with the shot, you could find yourself in trouble. So, before the point starts, have a look at where your opponents are standing, and then have an idea in your mind about what you're going to do with the first volley. And then stick with that idea.'

Don't be afraid, if you get a high ball, to smash the volley straight at an opponent at the net: 'Getting hit is an accepted part of the game.'

If both opponents are at the back of the court, you would tend to volley to the player with the weakest groundstrokes, and to the side on which they're weakest.

Your opponents are going to be moving around as much as possible, but you can't allow yourself to be distracted: 'You have to keep an eye on the ball at all times.'

Keep the ball as low as possible – this will help to prevent your opponents ripping groundstrokes past you.

Don't give your opponents a short ball: 'The last thing you want to do is to give your opponents the chance to step in and really take a big swing at their shot.'

MIXED DOUBLES

Daniela Hantuchova, who has a career grand slam in mixed doubles titles,
on 'HOW TO SUCCEED ON THE MIXED DOUBLES COURT' ...

Don't take it too seriously – the more fun you have on court, the more chance you have of winning matches: 'I think the reason I've had some success in mixed doubles is that I haven't cared at all whether I've won or lost. It can be stressful playing singles, as that's the competition that I really care about and want to do well in, but then when I'm playing mixed doubles it doesn't matter so much, and that means I'm going to be more relaxed. That's when I play well.'

It's key to choose a doubles partner that you get on with: 'If you feel relaxed on the court with them, you will have more success.'

For me it's important that the man doesn't smash the ball as hard as he can at the girl: 'I know what that's like, and it's not nice. I don't like it if a partner hits the ball hard at the girl. In fact, there have been a couple of times in my career that I've got pretty pissed when my partner has done that. I don't want to play with someone who thinks that's a good way of playing. Mixed doubles is meant to be fun.'

> **'If you feel relaxed, you will have more success.'**
> DANIELA HANTUCHOVA

Sania Mirza, who has won grand slam mixed doubles titles,
on 'HOW TO PLAY MIXED DOUBLES AS A WOMAN' ...

Prepare to be under attack throughout the match: 'Doubles teams are always going to attack the weaker of the two opponents, so in mixed doubles that probably means that the girl is going to be under attack most of the time.

So if the girl can deal with that, it's more than likely that her team will win. Whether a team wins or loses, that's usually up to how the girl plays, and not how the man plays.'

Don't be scared of getting hurt if the man hits the ball at you at full pace: 'At the pro level, there's a slam on the line, and the men certainly aren't going to take any pace off the ball and give you a softer shot. And, at an amateur level, maybe men are going to be just as competitive. And, anyway, it's not as if women hit the ball softly these days – your female opponent will also be hitting hard at you.'

John Lloyd, who won three grand slam mixed doubles titles,
on 'HOW TO BEHAVE ON THE MIXED DOUBLES COURT' ...

Don't play with your spouse: 'I really wouldn't advise anyone to play mixed doubles with their spouse, especially if both of you are competitive. I played a few matches with Chris [Evert, his former wife] – exhibitions and money matches – and it wasn't always easy. I think it's best, if you have a choice, to play with someone you're not emotionally involved with. If you play with your spouse, there's a danger that you're going to bring whatever's happening off the court on to it, and you're going to have a lot of baggage. If the match doesn't go your way, that's going to cause problems too.'

At an amateur level, don't blast the ball at your female opponent: 'It's different at a professional level now. The men aren't afraid of hitting the ball straight at the women. And the women aren't afraid of the men – as they're strong and great athletes. I think that's fine at a professional level, but not if you're playing at your local club. I wouldn't feel comfortable about going head-hunting and smacking any short ball straight at the woman.'

Jamie Murray, a former Wimbledon mixed doubles champion,
on 'HOW TO PLAY MIXED DOUBLES AS A MAN' ...

At a professional level, the man should hit the ball as hard at the woman as he does at the man: 'That seems sexist and wrong, but if you're taking this seriously, then that's the way you should do it. As a professional, you can make good money playing mixed doubles, so it's a cut-throat world.'

When serving to your female opponent, a spinning serve often works better than one hit at full power: 'I find that girls don't deal with the spin so well. They're more likely to return a hard serve which comes straight at them.'

Choose a partner who can hit big from the baseline, rather than a woman who likes to serve and volley: 'If your female partner is serve and volleying, it's easier for the man on the other side of the net to pick off the ball. I would rather have a partner who hits big from the baseline, someone who hits it hard enough to pass the guy at the net. If your male opponent is at the net he can intimidate and take control, and that's going to make it difficult. So if your partner can hold her own from the baseline and hit hard down the lines, and the guy doesn't know what's coming, that's ideal.'

Your partner will usually expect you to take the lead: 'If they do, make sure that you keep things simple so you both know what's expected of you.'

The more relaxed you feel, the better you will play: 'You're not always that intense playing mixed doubles. I always feel a bit more laid back playing mixed doubles than men's doubles, and play well for that reason.'

You don't have to flirt with your partner to be successful: 'However, it's important to keep your partner relaxed and enjoying it, as you're more likely to get better performances from them (although that's the same in men's doubles as well). There's a real skill to that, especially in professional tennis, as you won't play mixed doubles much – probably just four times a year at the grand slams and that's it. When I won Wimbledon in 2007 with Jelena Jankovic, we were enjoying it.'

COACHING

Serena Williams' coach, **Patrick Mouratoglou,**
on 'HOW TO PREPARE YOUR PLAYER FOR A MATCH' ...

Your player should have a clear idea about their opponent, and should be able to visualise how they play and behave. That information will often come from scouting their opponents: 'I've been scouting all the tour players for many years now. I've always considered that it is part of my coaching skill, as I want to prepare my player in the best possible way. Year after year, I have built my database with all the information that I consider decisive on every one of them. I use that information when I prepare my player before every match.'

Your message to your player should be clear: 'More than knowing how the opponent is playing, my client needs to have clear information on strengths and weaknesses, the most-used combination of shots, patterns on the major points, where the opponent serves and where he or she returns on both first and second serve. Before every match, I set up a strategy, taking into consideration both my player's game, strengths, favourite combinations, and the opponent's weaknesses. During the warm-up before the match we repeat, as an actor repeats his play, how we are going to play during the match.'

Trust in the numbers, not your emotions: 'I always like to take statistics of the matches, both of my player's and the future opponent's ones. Statistics don't lie. We can always have a wrong perception because we have emotions watching tennis. I love to challenge my feelings and my emotions by looking at the statistics and getting confirmation.'

Robert Lansdorp, who has coached Maria Sharapova, Pete Sampras and Tracy Austin, on 'HOW TO HAVE YOUR PLAYER COMPETING WITHOUT FEAR' ...

They need discipline. And they need it from a young age: 'I wasn't afraid to throw a four-year-old off the court once – he had a horrible attitude. He wasn't listening. With discipline you can make them do things that they had thought were impossible. I remember Maria Sharapova coming to me when she was 11. She was tough already at that age, but she needed guidance. Maria understood that if she didn't play the shots I wanted, she would be doing press-ups.'

Repetition, repetition, repetition: 'Have them hitting the same ball correctly over and over so it becomes completely automatic. That's a big part of being able to play without fear. It's about muscle memory. You work on their consistency, placement of the ball and power.'

Have your player practising under constant pressure: 'Tell them exactly what you want. And tell them what will happen if they don't do it: "You'll be doing 20 press-ups at the baseline." That will help to focus their minds. In matches, they will play without fear as they know that the shots work – they would have played them a thousand times on the practice court while under constant pressure.'

They need to be hitting the hell out of the ball. Not playing soft with lots of topspin. They need to be hitting harder and flatter, and deep into the court: 'How many pros play softly? All champions hit the hell out of the ball. You're not going to get that far by playing a ball with heavy topspin which clears the net by five or six feet. I call that "an academy ball". At almost every academy on earth, if you hit the ball in the net they tell them to start hitting the ball high over the net. That's nonsense. Most shots now on the pro tour are hit with some topspin, but they're clearing the net by just two or three feet. If you want to be great, you have to hit the ball hard. Have them hitting the ball harder and flatter from a young age, and they will be confident in the shot.'

Work hard on their second serve: 'A great way to develop their second serve is to hit them a high lob. They let the ball bounce, get set and then hit an overhead. Make them do 30 a day.'

Don't get hung up on surfaces: 'They say that you need to have grown up on clay courts to win the French Open. Well, that's the biggest bullshit story I've ever heard. Look at Michael Chang, who grew up on hard courts and then won the French Open at 17. Maria Sharapova grew up on hard courts and she won the French, too. Are you telling me that she suddenly became a clay-courter? No, of course she didn't. She was just hitting the ball hard.'

Nick Bollettieri, whose most famous students include Andre Agassi, the Williams sisters and Maria Sharapova, on 'HOW TO BE A WORLD-CLASS COACH' ...

Don't bullshit, don't give your player the Gettysburg Address: 'Don't make the mistake of talking too much to your player, or of talking too much to anybody. Boris Becker once said to me, "Nick, what makes you great is that you say just a few things, and then leave it at that."'

Show your player that you really care and believe in them, that this isn't just about getting paid at the end of a lesson: 'You have to make them think that they're better than they are, that this isn't about the money.'

Appreciate that no two players are the same, so you have to be flexible with how you coach your players, both mentally and physically. Listen to your player: 'It was Andre Agassi who taught me that. It shouldn't just be the coach telling the player what to do. You should be doing lots of listening as well.'

Never let your player settle for second best: 'Tell them that they're going out to be a winner. They might not always play their best tennis, but they are going to win.'

Roger Federer, Pete Sampras, Tim Henman and Sloane Stephens' former coach, Paul Annacone, on 'HOW TO COACH A FEMALE PLAYER' ...

Of course, there are differences between men's and women's tennis, but there are also many similarities: 'Many things are different – the game, for one. One similarity is that the women's game is getting much more athletic as well, and it's interesting to see how the women use their athleticism to suit their skills. And it's still a tennis court, it's still a game, and it's still about maximising your potential. But, most importantly, it's about maximising your average days and dealing with adversity and not letting that affect your self-belief, happiness or your goals.'

You won't be able to communicate with the player if you don't understand them: 'It helps to be aware of the generation, and to understand at least a little bit of what is going on with them. I really feel that if you are totally out of touch then you cannot have the same impact. The most important thing is for the player to feel at ease with the coach, so that the communication flows easily, and if that happens then you have should have a terrific partnership and a lot of fun.'

Sloane Stephens' former coach, Paul Annacone, on 'HOW TO PREPARE YOUR PLAYER FOR THE BIG OCCASION' ...

Make sure they understand their own game style, and how they play their best tennis: 'Keep the player oriented on process, not result.'

Make sure they have a clear idea of the best way to finish the points: 'What are their own strengths? And which patterns create ways to use those strengths to finish points?'

Accept imperfection: 'You are only as good as your average day. Be ready for adversity and react objectively, with clear thought and commitment to your own game plan.'

Stick to your game plan: 'Whether you win or lose, do so on your terms and evaluate your ability to stick to your own terms in the most pressure-filled times.'

Judy Murray, who has captained Britain's Fed Cup team,
on 'HOW TO COACH GIRLS' ...

Recognise that girls are more likely than boys to enjoy repetition, attention
to detail, sticking to a task and getting things right: 'Girls tend to be less
physical, less confident, less boisterous, less competitive than boys. With
boys, it's often about the competition, it's about obliterating a target or
smashing something very hard.'

Be careful how you speak to girls, who can quickly lose confidence. Try
using some gentle humour: 'In lots of ways, girls are easier to work with than
boys, but emotionally they can be trickier as they lose confidence much more
quickly than boys do. You have to be careful about how you phrase things,
and the language you use, and the times that you choose to speak to them. I
use a lot of humour but in a gentle way. I think the key with girls is to always
make them feel good about themselves. You need to find a way of bringing
a smile to their faces. I've always understood that if kids are having fun you
will get more out of them, they'll learn more quickly.'

Girls aren't as physically robust as boys – be wary of potential shoulder
injuries: 'Girls don't tend to be so strong in their shoulders and core. So they

will take a bit longer to get the hang of hitting serves and overheads. Serving is a significant part of the game, but you need to be sure that shoulders are stable before you are working on their serve. With all kids, it's important to teach technique that is bio-mechanically sound.'

There are going to be times when girls are hormonal and sulky – you'll have to find a way of getting through to them: 'This is one of the reasons why I think it's important for there to be more female coaches.'

Elena Baltacha, a former British No. 1 who set up her own academy, and who passed away at the age of 30 after losing a battle with liver cancer, on 'HOW TO COACH GIRLS' ...

Challenge them as much as you would challenge boys – it's a myth that girls don't want to be pushed as much as boys do: 'Girls are just as motivated, and as determined and as driven, as boys are.'

Judy Murray
on 'HOW TO STOP GIRLS FROM DROPPING OUT OF TENNIS' ...

Team competition is very important as you often find that girls drop out because their friends drop out: 'Maybe they don't enjoy it so much when their friends have stopped, and they're left just playing with the boys. And they're thinking that their friends are going to parties. What you need to do is make competition and the tennis environment more social. As well as team competition, girls also need a variety of competition formats, and competition that is fun.'

Having a female coach will encourage girls to carry on playing: 'In the early years, it's better for girls to have a female coach than a male coach, as women tend to have the softer skills which are needed for encouraging and nurturing, and that's especially true for those girls who lack confidence. To keep girls in the game, female coaches are invaluable.'

Even if girls have a male coach, you should also have a female around: 'As girls get older, and they need more discipline and a more hard-handed approach, male coaches could come into their own there. But if you're in an environment trying to produce a top player, you need to have a female around so the girl can go and speak to her if she has any worries or concerns. Teenage girls won't open up emotionally to men.'

Andy Murray's former coach Mark Petchey, on 'HOW TO COACH TEENAGE BOYS' ...

Don't try to turn them into monks: 'You've got to allow them their freedom. As a coach, you would be doing them a disservice as a human being if you told them, "You can't go out, you can't do this, you can't do that." By doing that, you introduce the forbidden-fruit syndrome. You say don't go out, then the night that they do go out, they go absolutely mental. Although with Andy, he never had that desire to go out and to drink. You have to allow teenagers to make some mistakes and to get it wrong in a controlled environment. I think a mistake we've made in Britain is that we've tried to turn our kids into nuns and monks at a very young age. They've been told that they have to be super-professional. But I think there's a balance to everything in life.'

Appreciate that you can't teach teenage boys if they don't want to learn: 'They have to want to learn.'

Rafa Nadal's uncle and coach, Toni, on 'HOW TO COACH SOMEONE IN YOUR FAMILY' ...

If you coach someone in your family, you should be able to be more honest with them as there shouldn't be the same concern about losing your job: 'It's not difficult to coach someone in your family. It's easier. When coaches are getting money from young players it's difficult, as they might not feel as though they can say exactly what they think, and what the players need to work on. They could just end up saying what the players want to hear because they don't want to lose the money from coaching them. For me, it's so much easier with Rafa as I'm part of the family, I'm the uncle, so I can say what I want. I can tell him what's good and what isn't so good.'

If you're normal and intelligent, you should be able to do a better job than someone outside the family. That's because you will care more than anyone else will: 'If your kids, nephews or nieces are good, and you can coach, I'm sure you can work with them so much better than other coaches would be able to. And there's a simple reason for that – you will have so much more interest in them. Sometimes when you work with someone in your family you are too strong and tough with them, or maybe you want it too much for them to be good, but when you look at the overall picture, I think it's better, and so much easier, to have a coach in the family.'

As a member of your family, the child should have respect for you: 'That's normal.'

Li Na, a multiple grand slam champion who in the past has employed her husband as her coach, **on 'HOW TO WORK WITH YOUR SPOUSE' ...**

Try not to argue too much – you need to find a balance: 'It's very tough. You're living together and your job is also together, on the court. It's very tough to find the balance between coach and spouse. You both feel a lot of pressure, so if you can, find a separate coach, too – that helped me a lot. We both felt much more relaxed and found life much easier.'

Appreciate that criticism will hurt more when it comes from your spouse: 'When you are playing badly on court and you look up at your coach/ husband in the stands, you'll still see him as your husband. If you then speak to him about your game, and he says something wrong, you think: "You're my husband, how can you say that?"'

Recognise that you could end up talking about tennis for 24 hours a day, and that's hard: 'In the evenings, you will carry on talking about tennis. Though sometimes it's the opposite – when we were fighting on court, we wouldn't talk at home, and that was tiring.'

Nick Bollettieri, legendary tennis coach,
on 'HOW TO TELL A YOUNG PLAYER THEY'RE NOT GOING TO MAKE IT' ...

You must always tell the truth: 'The problem is that coaches don't always tell their players that they're not going to make it, as they want to protect the money they're making from lessons. But you should always be honest.'

Tell the parents as soon as possible: 'Parents look at their child and think they can do just about anything. So it's not easy telling the parents that their child is not going to make it. Coaches are afraid to say anything to the parent. The parent might say, "What are you talking about?" and take the child to another coach. But it's up the coach to tell the truth.'

It's never been harder to tell whether someone is going to make it: 'It was easier in the past – with players like Andre Agassi, Pete Sampras, Jim Courier and Serena Williams – to work out whether a player was going to make it. But it's not so easy now. You want to look at a player's background, at their family, to find out things such as whether they are mortgaging the home for the child to play. Also, the whole world is playing now. In the 1970s, 1980s and early 1990s, it was essentially just five or six countries who were producing tennis players. With the entire world playing now, making predictions isn't easy.'

You have to be realistic: 'If two or three per cent of the students at the Nick Bollettieri Academy make it, I'm happy. And by making it I mean making good money, which means being in the top 60 or 70. Unless it looks as though you're going to be a superstar, a player will find it hard to get big sponsorship contracts. If a player isn't good enough, they should go to college.'

Magnus Norman, a former world No. 2 who went on to coach Stan Wawrinka,
on 'HOW TO GO FROM BEING A PLAYER TO A COACH' ...

Appreciate that it's harder mentally to watch matches from the side of the court than it is to play them yourself – that's because you can't do anything about what's happening out there: 'At the same time, try to enjoy watching your player on the court. I find Stan really enjoyable to watch.'

Don't feel as though you have to talk the whole time: 'Communication was difficult for me in the beginning. I wanted to say too much, and I was sometimes speaking at the wrong moments. Nowadays I choose when to speak and what to say. Sometimes the best thing you can do is to be quiet.'

If you've had some success as a player, there's no guarantee that you will be successful as a coach. However, use your experience to help the player you're working with: 'One advantage you have is that you'll be able to relate to how a player is feeling in different situations.'

Try to be a good listener rather than managing by fear: 'I have a vision about what is needed to climb higher in tennis, and I don't want to compromise on that. But it's also important that there's a trust between the coach and the player.'

If you want to succeed as a coach, be prepared to work long hours.

> 'There must be trust between the coach and the player.'
> MAGNUS NORMAN

Jo-Wilfried Tsonga, a former Australian Open finalist, on 'HOW TO CHOOSE YOUR COACH' ...

You need someone who will motivate you: 'You're alone on the court, every decision you take is down to you. So you need a coach to give you a way to think, and also to motivate you every day, and to make sure that your work is consistent.'

You're human, so it's important that you work with someone you like: 'I need a good relationship with my coach as otherwise I can't work.'

Stan Wawrinka, whose coach Magnus Norman helped him to win the 2014 Australian Open, on 'HOW TO KNOW IF YOU'VE GOT THE RIGHT COACH' ...

You need to feel as though you're constantly improving your game: 'That doesn't mean that you will get the results straight away, but you can think, "OK, we're going to work on something for the next few months, and improve every day." That's very important to me.'

You need to have respect for your coach: 'It's important to have a good relationship and to listen to them.'

Garbine Muguruza, who reached her first grand slam quarter-final at the 2014 French Open,
on 'HOW TO KNOW IF YOU HAVE A GOOD RELATIONSHIP WITH YOUR COACH' ...

You need to feel as though you have a connection: 'When he's motivated, you should be motivated. And when he's calm, you should be calm, too. He has to be able to give you the feelings, the emotions. Your coach needs to be able to get the message across well. If you don't have that sort of relationship, you can't work together.'

From the moment you wake up, your coach has to see how you feel, and has to know what he's going to tell you: 'They have to know what they can and can't say, and also the best time to say it – sometimes it's not the right time to say something.'

Your coach should feel comfortable criticising you. And you should feel comfortable listening to that criticism: 'Your coach should also be telling you what you're doing well, but you should welcome his criticisms as it's only by hearing what you are doing wrong that you can improve.'

Stan Wawrinka's coach, Magnus Norman,
on 'HOW TO CHANGE A PLAYER'S MENTALITY' ...

Appreciate that, at a high level, confidence is everything: 'Before you build up a player's confidence or belief, you have to read the player. It's different from player to player. Some players like to sit down and talk a lot. Some not.'

You can change a player's mentality quickly: 'But you need the player's trust. And you need the player to want to change.'

Working on a player's mental approach becomes more important as they improve and reach a higher level: 'When you coach younger players this is less important. Then you work with basic movement patterns as well as technical things. If you're coaching a player in the world's top 100 the mental game becomes more important.'

> 'You have to read the player.'
> **MAGNUS NORMAN**

Nick Bollettieri, founder of the world's most famous tennis academy, on 'HOW TO BE ALERT TO ILLEGAL COACHING' ...

Look out for a player's coach touching their nose, or their sunglasses. Or for other code and signals: 'Overall it's wrong, and you probably shouldn't be doing it, but I'm not going to lie about it – I've done it, and the majority of coaches give some direction from the stands. If I touched my nose, that could have been the code for, "Make sure you get your first serve in." If I touched my glasses, that could mean, "Hit a high ball." It absolutely still goes on, especially with Hawk-Eye, with players looking over at their coaches before deciding whether to challenge a line-call or not.'

But sometimes a coach doesn't help their player: 'Sometimes the sideline could be giving the wrong information. One year I was at the French Open, and I gave my player a card with all our codes on it. I said to her, "You look at the card, and if I scratch my nose do this, and if I touch my sunglasses do that." She kept looking up, but I had left the card back at the hotel, so I had to sit there all match without moving. She won the match, though, so it was OK.'

Andy Murray and Laura Robson's former coach, Miles Maclagan, on 'HOW TO STAY MOTIVATED ON THE PRACTICE COURT' ...

By having a clear idea of your game style you will know what kind of shots you will need to fulfil that vision and then dedicate the bulk of your time to those areas: 'As a rule, if you can't do it on the practice court, don't expect to be able to do it on the match court.'

Have a definite, simple purpose for each session and drill: 'I would recommend focusing on one specific at a time. Motivation on the practice court comes from having clear, achievable objectives in mind. If you're just randomly hitting balls, chances are you won't stay focused for long and won't get the maximum gain from your session.'

You should always be looking to improve, but you also have to be sensible with your goals, targets and drills: 'Be realistic. If you've been playing for many years and have never hit a topspin backhand in your life, going out for hours and hours to hit topspin backhands is probably not the most productive use of your time and is probably going to sap your energy. You will find it more beneficial to improve what you have.'

Choose your practice partner well – someone who also wants to be out there, who hits the ball well, and has high energy levels: 'If you're dragging someone out to the court who doesn't really want to play, that's not going to help your level. There are certain players, on the tour and at all levels, who, although they are great players, aren't ideal if you're trying to get a bit of rhythm.'

'Motivation comes from having clear, achievable objectives.'
MILES MACLAGAN

Use targets: 'This will help you to focus and picture exactly what sort of shots you're trying to hit.'

Introduce some competition into the practice: 'Even the simplest of drills can be made competitive by using targets or seeing who can keep the ball in play longest (remembering to keep a clear objective in mind), and hopefully that will raise concentration and intensity. Whether doing drills or playing practice sets, why not put a little something on it, maybe the loser buys the drinks afterwards or pays for the court time? However, there are times when I would advise against scoring, such as when you're working on something technical or trying to improve a specific shot. For example, you may be trying to get more angle or depth on a certain shot, so if you missed wide or long occasionally that wouldn't be a problem. It would be counter-productive for you to be worried about losing points when the aim is to experiment and push the boundaries.'

Mix it up, and try to replicate what you would be doing in a match: 'Around 60 to 70 per cent of a pro's practice is going through the basics. You're going to hit your forehands and backhands cross-court, and you definitely want to make sure that you hit some serves in every session. Sometimes I like to break up the serving. In a match you obviously only serve every alternate game s o there is a time for hitting serves for 20 or 30 minutes, but there are also times for hitting 10 to 15 serves, then going on to do another drill, and then going back to hitting serves, replicating a match situation – the aim being to keep a very high focus level in order to get the most from the exercise.'

If there is a specific area or element of your game that you're looking to improve, by all means spend more time on it, but be wary of overdoing it: 'Doing one exercise for too long will dampen your focus after a while and may risk injury. Most people prefer practising the things they're good at, and it's important to do so, as it will help lift your confidence and after all, it's your strengths that that will get the X in the win column.'

Mark Petchey, former player, coach and now TV commentator, on 'HOW TO STOP YOUR PLAYER FROM FEELING BORED ON THE PRACTICE COURT' ...

You need to find ways of practising the same shot in a different way, and making it fun: 'That's not always easy to do. So you are somewhat reliant on the player's appetite for repetition because tennis is all about repetition. If you can hit the ball over the net more times than your opponent can, you're going to win. If you've got the fire in the belly to do that, you've got a great shot at being a great player. There are unfortunately no circus tricks that you can bring to a practice court that make it fun for the sake of making it fun.'

> 'If you've got money on it, it gets more exciting.'
> MARK PETCHEY

Tennis players are naturally competitive so competitive drills get their juices flowing more than any others: 'If you put something on it, it gets exciting. That goes on a lot. I've lost a lot of money doing that. Sometimes, though, a coach shouldn't be making a bet as you think you'll win and that could put the player in a bad mood.'

Accept that some days you won't get much from your player: 'So you say to them, "Let's do slice backhands or drop shots" – something you know they will enjoy. You have to think, "OK, let's try to maximise the hour we're going to get out of you today." That's one of the key things as a coach. You can start the day by saying, "I want you out there for five hours today, I'm going to push you through the wall, you're going to hurt, you're going to burn." There are times for that. But there are also times when you think, "Do you know what? Today it's just not happening." You write it off. You need to be effective for a shorter period of time and then just go. In the longer term, that's more beneficial.'

Don't always try to make practice sessions fun as then you could be ignoring what they need to work on: 'You could make a practice session fun for someone by getting them to hit volleys and half-volleys all day long, when you know that will be just five per cent of their match. Don't ignore the cross-court forehands and service returns, which they're going to do 80 per cent of the time.'

If your player is looking bored, have a chat with them to work out what the reason is: 'There could be personal reasons. Being a tennis coach is often more psychological than anything else. You need to have a good honest chat. Are they copping out? Or are you boring them? Are they tired of hearing your voice? If you look at tennis as a whole, why is it that coaches seem to have a shelf life of between two and three years before they get rotated? Because that coach is saying that same thing a lot of the time, and it's right that they're saying that, but eventually the player says, "I don't want to hear its any more." But that doesn't mean that, as a coach, you should just say something they want to hear, something that sounds good. You have to be true to yourself.'

Tim Henman and Donna Vekic's former coach, David Felgate, on 'HOW TO BE A GOOD COACH' ...

The biggest mistake you can make as a coach is not being tough enough and not sticking to your beliefs. Don't let the player take control: 'That can be a problem with some coaches. Suddenly the player becomes good and they start to call the shots. In my opinion, that's not the right way around. Clearly, a player evolves and your relationship evolves, and you're working together, but you have to stick to your principles. Don't let outside influences change those. If you're worrying about losing your job, and you think that calling the shots could be a problem, you cease to have an impact as a coach. Coaches are protecting their situation, as the players are the paymaster, but if you allow that to happen, you compromise your principles.'

When you're watching your player on court, try to keep your emotions and feelings hidden: 'Sometimes that's difficult, if there's some anger, and you let that show. Or if you're pleased with how a situation is going, and you're trying to stay balanced, sometimes that's not easy. But it's best to keep your thoughts and emotions to yourself.'

Olga Morozova, a former French Open and Wimbledon finalist, who has worked with **Svetlana Kuznetsova**, on 'HOW TO BE A GREAT COACH' ...

Don't be too pushy or selfish or egotistical – you have to know when to stand back: 'As a coach, you need knowledge and ideas. But all coaches, and especially those who were good players before, need to step back a little. Tennis players are supposed to make their own decisions on the court. If the coach is too pushy, then it will not be the player's decision', it will be the decision of the coach. Then, when a player needs to make a decision on court at the important time, they won't be able to do it. You have to be in the shadow of your player, and it has to be clear to everyone that it's the player who is making the decisions.'

Don't be afraid to learn from anyone and everyone: 'Sometimes the good coaches learn from players, not from themselves, though you still need to have your own vision.'

It's very important for the player to know that, whatever happens on the court, you are with them, and will do whatever's necessary to make things work: 'You have to be 100 per cent with them. You don't have your life any more, when you're with them – you have to be there for them.'

Have a Plan B: 'You're supposed to be a psychologist sometimes, and sometimes you are supposed to be an expert in fitness. If a player didn't sleep well or has a stomach upset, they won't be able to play in a certain way on the court, so you need to have a second plan for them in that situation.'

You have to be ready for everything the player does: 'You not only have to plan for today, you have to plan for the whole year.'

Be a good listener: 'There is such pressure on tennis players that you have to give them the opportunity to say whatever worries them and then to have a nice or patient answer.'

THE AGES OF TENNIS

PARENTING

Roger Federer's mother **Lynette** on 'HOW TO BE A GOOD TENNIS PARENT' ...

It's important that your child enjoys the game and isn't forced into it: 'I believe a child chooses tennis because he or she is attracted to and fascinated by the sport, and that could be through the parents, friends or family.'

Discipline is part of the game: 'If a child wants to play tennis, then it means he or she has to behave properly at practice and during matches. This is not always an easy task as emotions play a big role, influencing behaviour and results. If your child is misbehaving, I would not intervene during practice, but would discuss it with the coach and try to identify why your child is behaving like that. Bad behaviour during practice can also be a result of a lack of interest, poor tennis coaching, or a child having a bad day at school or at home. I would also speak to the child about his or her behaviour. In Roger's case, when his behaviour was poor during a match, I told him he was inviting or asking his opponent to beat him.'

Parents should go with the flow. Don't be too ambitious for your child. And don't intervene too much: 'The progress of a child can differ in the same age group – due to size, maturity and other factors – so some children are going to progress faster than others at the beginning of their junior career and will later be surpassed by those who were weaker at an earlier age. Our role as the parent of a junior is to ensure they attend their practice (though not to stand behind the fence all the time), accompany them to their matches, motivate them and comfort them when necessary and, most importantly of all, to ensure that they enjoy the game, and not to put pressure on your child in any way.'

A child can start playing tennis from the age of three or four in a playful manner: 'Roger started at the age of three because my husband and I spent weekends at the tennis club and he just picked up the racket and loved playing against the wall, and at home against the cupboard. Whenever we could we played on court with him. He could play for hours by himself. Later he played with friends on the road with a mini-tennis net and a soft ball.'

It's not easy to say how you can help your child find the right coach: 'We were very fortunate that we had a good system in Switzerland. If a child was talented, they were selected with the best of their age group and had good regional coaches. We were also lucky to have very good coaches at our local club.'

A parent's role can be very important in the success of a junior: 'Without the support and guidance of a parent it will be difficult for a junior to succeed.'

Andy and Jamie Murray's mother Judy
on 'HOW TO DO THE BEST FOR YOUR CHILDREN' ...

You need to let go a little at some stage: 'You never know if you've made the right decision but you have to apply common sense and go with your gut feeling a lot of the time. It's not that you hand over everything, but you have to try to find the right places or the right people and you have to trust them. You have to keep an eye on it, you can't just hand your child over to a tennis academy in Barcelona [Andy Murray trained at an academy in the city] and say, "I'll be back for you in four months." You have to make sure they are doing the right things.'

You don't know it all – get some help by talking to other parents: 'I've heard enough horror stories about people who have got it wrong. You have to understand that you don't know enough about it to think you can do it all yourself and so you have to find the right people to help you.'

Ana Ivanovic, a former world No. 1 and French Open champion,
on 'HOW TO HELP YOUR CHILD GET THE MOST OUT OF THEIR TENNIS' ...

It's a very bad idea for anyone to coach their child, as it then becomes difficult for the parent to separate parenting and coaching: 'And it's very hard for the kids, too. All of a sudden, kids don't want to see their parents as they've had enough of tennis and practising. For parents, it's going to be hard to educate their kid and talk about anything other than tennis. If a kid has to listen to a parent talking all the time about tennis, and then talking about life in general, the kid is going to be thinking, "OK, just leave me to live my life a little bit as I don't want you to influence every part of it." Coaching your child can only hinder them.'

> **'Most kids just want freedom.'**
> ANA IVANOVIC

Parents should never try to live their dreams through their kids, and make them play a sport they don't want to play: 'I've seen that over the years, and it's just wrong.'

The most important thing is to make sure that your child wants to be on court, and takes pleasure from playing tennis: 'There are so many talented kids out there who, at an early age, have been forced to train too much by their parents, and they start to hate tennis. That's because, all of a sudden, it's something they have to do. Most kids just want freedom. They just want to play. Especially when they're young, I think they just want to think that they're playing a game, and that it's nothing serious. So don't force them to practise a certain number of hours or anything like that.'

Kids should be encouraged just to play points, rather than doing drills: 'They should be having a fun and interesting time on court – they shouldn't be drilling or grinding as then they could lose the desire to play.'

Don't put pressure on your child to succeed. Just support them: 'My parents never put pressure on me. They just talked about how important it is to be happy, and to behave well on the court. For them those were the most important things. Looking back, that was great as so many parents these days put so much pressure on their kids. What they should be doing is offering unconditional support as that's what kids need. Yes, you should show your kid the way. You need to give them discipline so that they respect the time and money that has gone into tennis, so they recognise that they have been given an opportunity to be on court. But that's not the same as putting pressure on them. Every tennis player needs a supportive family.'

Allow your child to make their own decisions: 'There are so many cases when parents are very, very controlling. That's so bad. The parents should be there to make sure that there are the right people around their child. But then they should leave it up to their kid and the coach to play and learn and to go into the details.'

Greg Rusedski, a former US Open finalist and world No. 4,
on **'HOW TO AVOID BEING A NIGHTMARE TENNIS PARENT'** ...

Make sure your child has good values: 'Sometimes you get cheating in junior tournaments – that happens in every single country in the world. Your child has to understand that, in the long run, cheating isn't going to work.'

Appreciate that your child won't win every tournament they play: 'There's only one winner at the end of each week. There are going to be times when the child loses a lot of close matches, and the parent and coach have to make sure that the development is monitored.'

Understand that, if your child is phenomenal at 12 or 14, that doesn't guarantee any future success: 'And one child's goal will differ from another's. Some kids might want to use tennis to help them get a university degree. Others might want to get a pro career. But kids can't really make those decisions until they're 16, 17, 18 years old. If I hadn't been up to a certain level at the age of 17, I would have got a university scholarship in America.'

Talk to the coach and make sure everyone is giving the same message to the child: 'Parents have to work in conjunction with the coach. You can't have one message from the coach and another one from the parent – they have to be passing on the same message. You have to communicate together. Communication is so important.'

Don't let your child take the easy route, especially if they want to play at the highest level: 'The child has to understand what's expected of them.'

Understand that as your child gets older, he or she may lose his or her passion for tennis, or they could get injured: 'It's a long voyage and lots of things can happen.'

Serena and Venus Williams' father, Richard,
on 'HOW TO INSTIL THE RIGHT VALUES IN YOUR TENNIS-PLAYING CHILDREN' ...

Players need to respect themselves. And also have the respect of their families: 'But the respect of other people? Venus and Serena don't give a damn about that.'

Young tennis players need to know that there is a world outside tennis: 'Tennis is just a game. I'm not proud of what my daughters have done in tennis. I'm proud of my daughters for who they are, and for what they've achieved outside tennis. Too many players in tennis, these champions, don't know anything outside tennis. They haven't been to college, tennis is all they know, and what else can they do? They stop playing and then they become coaches or TV announcers, they stay in tennis. They can't do anything else. Most players can't see that there's a life beyond the baseline, that the baseline is the baseline. My daughters have been to college, they have an education, and they're not going to be broke.'

Wimbledon referee Andrew Jarrett
on 'HOW TO COPE WHEN YOUR CHILD IS HAVING A TANTRUM ON COURT' ...

Your child needs to know that, by behaving badly, they're helping their opponent: 'If I was the opponent of the child throwing a tantrum, I would be thrilled and delighted. If I see my opponent throwing a tantrum, I know they're not concentrating. They're not focusing on the match, they're rattled, they're upset. That's great news. So the child having the tantrum needs to understand that, and to cut that nonsense out as soon as possible. They're not doing what they're supposed to be doing, which is trying to win a tennis match.'

Occasionally you might hear of a parent walking on court to intervene saying, 'Give me your racket, you're not going to play for a week... for a year,' whatever. But that's just one way of dealing with this: 'There's no hard and fast rule. Everyone's different. You have to look at the whole situation and try to find the best solution. It's not easy. It can be very inflammatory and can lead to a breakdown in the relationship.'

First and foremost, parents should be parents, and so shouldn't intervene in any situation: 'Ask for assistance. That could mean officials, or coaches, or other people who are working with that player. Parents should be in the background, backing up that communal effort. It's difficult when parents step over that line and try to take on additional roles such as being a coach. It's not impossible. There are some great examples of people who have crossed that line and done it very successfully. But there are more examples when it hasn't been so successful and the result is a breakdown in relations. That's a shame because the parent-child relationship is a very special one, and I think that should be protected.'

Jo Durie, a former world No. 4,
on 'UNDERSTANDING WHY YOUR CHILD IS MISBEHAVING ON COURT' ...

You need to stop the tantrum first. Tell your child that if they don't stop throwing their racket or swearing, you will ban them from playing tennis: 'If the child really loves tennis, they'll stop doing it. I think you need to be quite hard on your child because smashing rackets and swearing is not acceptable.'

Ask yourself whether your child is behaving like that because there's so much pressure on them: 'Their desperation to get the win sometimes means they can't control their emotions. You absolutely want to see some passion and fight but you don't want to see it ticking over into desperation. You also don't want to see them going into a mini tantrum about not getting their own way.'

Annabel Croft, a former British No. 1, on 'HOW TO ENJOY TENNIS AS A FAMILY' ...

Play mixed doubles and mix up ages and standards of play: 'Playing mixed doubles as a family is one of my favourite things. One of the most amazing things about tennis is that you can involve players of all ages. There aren't many other sports that allow you to do that. On a tennis court, you can have a grandfather in his 70s playing alongside his 11-year-old grandchild. That's really sweet. If you swap around after a few games, it's fun and it keeps everything going. I like to mix up ages and standards of play, to make sure that one person doesn't end up feeling they've lost out every time. You should avoid putting strong players together.'

Don't make it too pressured – but as kids get older, there will be probably be some hairy moments along the way: 'Rackets will be thrown – that's the tennis equivalent of throwing the Monopoly board into the air. It can get tense with pre-teens. One way to avoid that is to make sure that everyone has a chance to partner the best players. But part of what tennis is about is learning how to deal with those emotions.'

You can start playing with the kids from a young age: 'I've been hitting with my kids since they were tiny, since the age of two or three.'

> 'Rackets will be thrown – it can get tense.'
> **ANNABEL CROFT**

You don't have to play sets to have fun. Drills can be fun, too, though it helps if there's a competitive element: 'You will find that the level goes up. You raise the intensity level, but you're not putting pressure on anyone. You're not just aimlessly hitting balls.'

Jo Durie on 'HOW TO INTRODUCE YOUR CHILD TO TENNIS' ...

There isn't a right age for kids to start playing; they should start whenever they feel ready. When they do start it's important for them to use soft balls and large rackets: 'This allows the child to swing as madly and as hard as they like without it being dangerous. It also means they can have as much fun as possible which is so important.'

Make sure your child spends plenty of time hitting balls over nets and against walls: 'This gives them a feel of the ball and gives them a chance to practise their swing.'

Kim Clijsters, a former world No. 1 and US Open and Australian Open champion, on 'HOW TO COMBINE MOTHERHOOD AND TENNIS' ...

Just do it: 'I spoke to Evonne Goolagong [Cawley] about what it was like winning Wimbledon as a mother. She said to me, "Yeah, you should do it – you go out and play and if you lose, you lose, and the next day you're home taking care of the kid." And that's how it felt for me. OK, there were days when it was hard, but I just got on with it.'

Try to forget your defeats quickly: 'There were times when I was upset after losing a match and my daughter Jada came over and within a minute I was laughing because she was being silly. It made me realise, "Who cares about the match?" I worked hard to achieve and to do the best that I could. I was brought up to think that I shouldn't stress out too much about a tennis match. Try to learn from it, and don't think that it's the end of the world if you lose, because it really isn't. It would be embarrassing to think like that.'

JUNIORS AND TEENAGERS

Maria Sharapova, who won Wimbledon at 17, on 'HOW TO BECOME A CHAMPION' ...

Don't have any regrets – it's important to give everything you have, and to commit to the sport: 'If you're thinking of doing something, really go for it. If you have any incredible opportunities or chances, you really want to take them, because you don't want to look back after however many years and think that you weren't there when you wanted to be, whether that's physically or mentally.'

From a young age, you need discipline and to make big sacrifices: 'The moments you look back to – if you are victorious – are the moments when you really knew that it was tough, and when you had to push yourself. When you faced adversity and showed that you can dig deep. I look back and think, "Yeah, that was tough, but I got through it." Friends would have sleepovers, and I would have a tournament, and wouldn't be able to join them. As a young girl, that's a huge deal. Even to this day, my friends have vacations in the summer – they're going off on holidays – and I'm playing the French Open and Wimbledon back-to-back so my holiday doesn't come until November when the season's over. Maybe my life isn't as normal as my friends' lives, but the great thing is that they respect that.'

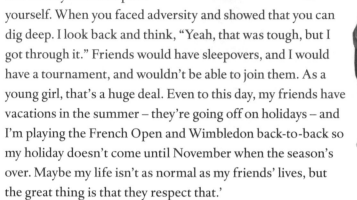

There will be good experiences and not-so-good experiences – try to learn from everything and to become mentally stronger: 'It's a lot of fun, but it's all a rollercoaster. There are going to be lots of ups and downs. Take it all in. I hope that I've grown as a person and as a player during my career. I've been through so much, on and off the court, and I've become stronger mentally and emotionally.'

Novak Djokovic's coach, Marian Vajda,
on 'HOW TO HAVE THE BEST START TO YOUR TENNIS LIFE' ...

Be happy – at the beginning there shouldn't be too much emphasis on winning: 'Tennis is fantastic for the body. You're going to release your hormones and adrenalin, and you're going to be happier. It helps you to become a better person. It's a game so you get a lot of good feelings when you win, but also just through playing.'

If you want to end up playing professional tennis, you probably need to pick up a racket before your sixth birthday: 'Becoming a tennis player is a process and you can't rush that, so you have to be committed from a young age, and it has to be a pleasure most of the time. I remember when I was a boy I was drawn to the sport. I was almost eating all the tennis results.'

You never want to lose your passion for tennis. But if you want to be competitive – whether you want to be a professional or just a better club player – it's no longer just about the fun: 'If you decide to take it seriously, you have to practise more and more. That's when it becomes difficult for young players as they have to follow the same routine every day.'

If you're getting angry on the court, shouting and throwing your racket, you need to have a good look at yourself: 'That could be a sign that you shouldn't be playing. Or it could be a sign that you're just very determined to win. This is where you need help from a coach. Maybe the coach should say, "Look, we have to talk about this, it's not nice to see this from a young player – even though we see this from some of the top guys in tennis, you shouldn't be doing it. You shouldn't always follow the example of the top players." If a player is talented, maybe the coach should give him a bit more room to express himself. On the other hand, perhaps a coach should be telling him to be more disciplined and to keep his focus.'

You need a good sporting culture around you: 'If you are to do well, you need to be in a healthy environment, and you need the parents and the coaches to be working together.'

Eugenie Bouchard, a former junior Wimbledon champion who reached her first senior grand slam final at the 2014 Wimbledon Championships,

on 'HOW TO MAKE THE TRANSITION FROM THE JUNIORS TO THE SENIORS' ...

Accept that your social life is going to take a hit: 'If you want to play tennis professionally, you can't do all the normal things that teenagers do. You have to accept there are sacrifices. If you're going to succeed, you have to make a decision and stick with it. Still, that doesn't mean that you have to stop having fun altogether.'

Playing tennis is a job. It's good to have some friends on the tour, but you will probably only have a limited friendship circle: 'It's just not easy to be friends with a lot of the girls when you're going to be competing against them each week.'

In the juniors, you can get away with losing your concentration for a while. But that's not going to happen in the seniors: 'No one's going to give up on a point in the seniors. While you have to step up physically to play tennis in the seniors, probably the biggest difference between junior and senior tennis is the mental toughness.'

Be patient: 'It's going to take some time establishing yourself in the seniors. You have to remember that there's a long way to go.'

Before you go full-time in senior tennis, play just a few senior tournaments, so you're combining junior and senior tennis: 'That will make it easier to go from one to the other.'

Filip Peliwo, who won the junior titles at Wimbledon and the US Open, and who held the world junior No. 1 ranking, on **'HOW TO DEVELOP YOUR TENNIS CAREER'** ...

Make friends, because you're going to see the same players all the time. Have fun with your life on the road and enjoy what you do. You should make sure you have a good balance between tennis and your personal life: 'The worst mistake you can make is to focus too much on the game and burn out before you reach your true potential. That being said, you do have to make sure to put in enough work and not spend too much time on your personal off-court life.'

> **'You have to learn how to deal with pressure.'**
> **FILIP PELIWO**

To help you stay disciplined, remember that you're getting to experience things that your friends who don't play tennis never will: 'So appreciate what you do, the places you go to, and the people you meet. You know that what you are working for will pay off eventually, and that keeps you motivated to stay disciplined.'

Constantly strive to improve and develop your game, and eventually it will all come together, but don't put too much pressure on yourself as that runs the risk of burn-out: 'It's extremely important to learn how to deal with pressure and expectation to a certain point. You have to be able to bring out your best game in the tight moments, when the whole match can be decided by only a few points. You must also be able to focus on your game rather than the result, and all of the expectations and pressure that come with success. That is what separates a lot of the top players from the rest. That being said, it's important to keep in mind that being a junior is the first step in a long tennis career, it's where you build your confidence, and that's why it's important that you don't put too much pressure on yourself. Once you have had success as a junior, you must be able to shift your focus on to the next level and remember all the lessons you learned, which can be translated to the pro tour.'

Make the most of any opportunities to practise with players on the senior tour – there's so much you can learn from them. Juniors can be erratic – you can win matches by being consistent, and by making a few extra shots: 'But if you are working towards making that transition to the pros then I think you should be concentrating on improving your game for when you start playing against guys on the tour. You don't want to be winning in juniors with a game style that won't get you anywhere on the professional tour. In senior tennis, you have to go for your shots a bit more, and try to win the point rather than just trying to get your shots in the court, as that won't get you too many free points.'

But be alert to the danger of getting ahead of yourself: 'You can't only think about what the future holds – you have to also think about winning the matches you are playing now.'

Serena Williams, arguably the greatest female player of all time, on 'WHAT JUNIORS MUST DO IF THEY WANT TO END UP PLAYING AT THE GRAND SLAMS AND BECOMING CHAMPIONS' …

Believe in yourself: 'Dream big. You've got to have big dreams and to think to yourself, "I can do it".'

There's no easy route to success: 'You have to train hard [if you're going to achieve your dreams].'

'You've got to have big dreams.'
SERENA WILLIAMS

Donna Vekic, who was ranked in the top 100 when she was 16,
on 'HOW TO BE A TEENAGE TENNIS STAR' ...

Work hard and stay humble: 'Even though I'm in the top 100 I'm still very far from my final goal, which is being No. 1. The biggest mistake you can make as a teenage tennis player is to think you have already made it and that you don't have to work hard any more. That's totally wrong, as the real hard work comes now.'

Don't let yourself be influenced by what others are saying: 'I'm always the one with the highest expectations, but I try not to care what others say. It's not always easy but it's the best thing to do.'

Older players can get nervous when playing against teenagers. So you have to use that advantage early in the match and make them work for it: 'Older players are obviously more physically, mentally, tactically and psychologically developed but sometimes younger players don't have any pressure on them; so they can be totally relaxed.'

Your phone will help you to avoid boredom, loneliness and homesickness on the tour: 'My phone is my best friend when I'm on tour. Sometimes it's not easy being away from home, but it's all part of the job. You can't just have the good stuff.'

In this world it's very hard to associate with people who aren't tennis players: 'People who don't play tennis don't really understand what you're going through so you don't have much in common.'

You need to be able to trust your coach to put together the right schedule for you so that you don't risk burn-out.

Martina Hingis, who won the women's title at Wimbledon at the age of 16,
on 'HOW TO BE A TEENAGE PRODIGY' ...

Once you start having a nice lifestyle from tennis, there are going to be lots of distractions all around you, but you need to stay disciplined: 'On tour, you're going to beautiful places and staying in five-star hotels, and everyone at the tournament is trying to make sure you have a great experience, and that everything is the best for you. It's a nice life, but it's also very comfortable, so you have to watch out to make sure you don't become too comfortable. You can get lazy. You need the people around you to keep on pushing you. If you stop working, and stop doing all the things you need to, your level is going to drop. It's almost harder staying at a high level than it is getting there in the first place.'

Sometimes it's best if you think your early success is normal: 'When I won Wimbledon at 16, the victories felt so normal. It was a special moment, but I was the No. 1 seed, so I was supposed to win. I was used to winning. I had the confidence in myself, and winning just became the normal thing to do.'

Don't put too much pressure on yourself – remember that if it doesn't happen for you now you're still got plenty of time left: 'I never struggled to deal with it all because I thought, as a teenager, there was so much more time to go. If I didn't succeed that year, I felt as though I would have many more chances.'

Michael Chang, who won the French Open at 17,
on 'HOW TO PREPARE FOR A TENNIS CAREER' ...

Expose yourself to pressure: 'Every ambitious young player is working on their game, but the best thing a teenager can do is to go out there and learn how to play under pressure. You have to go out there and play against your peers, against the opponents you don't want to play, against the players who make you uncomfortable. Some juniors don't want to play against each other because they don't want to lose. But you need to learn about the pressure from your opponent, and the pressure of expectation – the pressure from yourself, from being watched by spectators and by a television audience, from the press, from the people travelling with you, from your friends and family, from the country. If you're playing tennis without pressure, you're doing yourself a disservice.'

So play against your peers as much as possible: 'I was blessed that I was part of such a talented generation in the States, which included Andre Agassi, Pete Sampras and Jim Courier. We were always playing against one another in junior tournaments, and no one wanted to be at the back of the pack. You knew that you had to work hard, and to fight, as otherwise you would be at back. Of course, the pressure you feel in the juniors is different to the pressure of being at senior grand slams. But all of us had learnt in the juniors how to win, and we all won senior grand slams at a young age.'

No tennis champion ever did anything on his own – it's impossible. So you need a good group around you: 'There will be a lot of people with a lot of opinions. When you're winning, everyone will want to be your friend. But when you're losing and having a tough time, that's when you'll discover who really cares and who has your best interests at heart. You need people who will make you feel positive, and who will encourage you. That's the way to grow.'

OLDER PLAYERS

Kimiko Date-Krumm, who in 2013 at the age of 42 became the oldest woman to win a match during the Australian Open, on 'HOW TO PLAY GREAT TENNIS IN YOUR 40s' ...

Make the most of your opponent's nerves: 'When you're playing someone 20 years younger, they will be expected to win the match, and so they might get very nervous. You have to take advantage of that, and perhaps find a way of putting even more pressure on them. You have to make the most of your experience – if you don't get the mental side right, you won't stand much of a chance.'

Get plenty of sleep: 'When I was in my 20s, seven hours' sleep a night was enough, and I would wake up and be ready to go. But I definitely need more sleep in my 40s. I like to sleep a lot, for at least eight hours a night, and sometimes nine or ten hours. I sleep more during tournaments.'

Don't eat cake and ice cream the night before a match: 'The older you get, the more carefully you have to think about what you eat, as your body takes longer to recover. So before a match, or before a training day, eat a lot of carbohydrates, and afterwards you need a lot of protein. It's OK to sometimes have chocolate, cake and ice cream, but only occasionally, and not when you're getting ready to compete.'

You won't be as strong as you once were, so there's no point trying to overpower your younger opponents: 'You have to think about other ways to win. So I mix it up, I use angles, change the pace, drop in a short ball or come to net.'

No one likes to lose, but learn not to care so much about the result: 'Just enjoy being at tournaments and competing.'

Virginia Wade
on 'HOW TO BE A DANGEROUS OPPONENT IN YOUR 40s' ...

Take yourself a little less seriously: 'If you start thinking that you're still the same player that you were ten years ago, you're setting yourself up to fail. But if you think that you're doing the best you can at that time, then that's just fine. Some people take themselves way too seriously. You just think "oh please". You're hanging on to your game because you're making the most of the opportunities you have. But you're not going to be beating everyone in sight.'

You have to constantly look for ways to adapt and improve: 'You have to get a little smarter, and do things you weren't doing before.'

Don't over-play, or push yourself too hard, as you will injure yourself: 'As you get older, you will take longer to recover from matches.'

Jonas Bjorkman, a former doubles world No. 1 who has coached Andy Murray,
on 'HOW TO ENJOY YOUR TENNIS IN MIDDLE AGE' ...

Don't have any expectations – certainly don't think you are going to move as quickly, or hit the ball as hard, as you once did: 'If you start thinking like that, you're not going to have fun. You have to accept you're going to be a little slower. I think once the ball comes to you it should actually be easy to play. The most important thing is to be relaxed, and then you will have a lot of fun.'

MISCELLANEOUS

Dmitry Tursunov,
who has been ranked in the world's top 20,
on 'HOW TO SMASH A RACKET' ...

Embrace it: 'I think more of the top players should be encouraged to smash rackets. They are trying to show how intense and passionate they are on court, and what better way to do that than destroying rackets?'

Don't ever throw the racket: 'If you hold on to it, you feel more in control, it's really *you* smashing the racket, you can feel it breaking, you can feel the vibrations and the force down your arm. Also, if you throw your racket across the court, and it doesn't break, and there's only a scratch on it, then you are going to feel like an idiot when you walk over to pick it up.'

Breaking a racket on grass earns you extra style points: 'I'm impressed by anyone who can break a racket on a grass court. That's really manly, but it's difficult. You could just end up with a big divot in the grass. I remember doing it once on grass when I was really pissed off, and it ended up sticking out of the grass like a spear.'

Practise, practise, practise: 'You have to get your racket-smashing right on the practice court. You don't want to look stupid when playing matches.'

Deal with the remorse: 'Afterwards, you feel a bit sorry that you've done it, and you're like, "Yeah, I'll make it up to you darling, my little racket." But the racket is broken and you know that it's never going to be the same again.'

Goran Ivanisevic, a former Wimbledon champion,
on 'WHY SMASHING RACKETS IS A GOOD THING' ...

Ignore the boos from the crowd: 'The people booing you, they've probably been complaining that people haven't been breaking rackets, and that tennis is too boring, and there are no characters. Then they're not happy when people are breaking rackets. I mean, what the f***. They should make up their minds. If you want to break a racket, you should be allowed to break a racket. If, like me, you have a talent for it, you can break your racket on any surface – I can break a racket on water.'

You have to move on immediately – break the racket and then forget about it: 'It's not a problem smashing rackets. If you want to smash the racket, smash the racket, and take a new one, but forget about the one you've just smashed. A lot of the time, I would smash the racket and then I would spend the next five games thinking about the racket. I was thinking, "Why did I break that racket? Should I have broken that racket?" That was my mistake, thinking about it too much. If you want to break the racket, just break the motherf***** and stop thinking about it. Take a new one and just forget about it.'

But make sure you don't smash all the rackets in your bag: 'I was the first person to lose a match because I had smashed everything and run out of rackets. It wasn't that satisfying. The moment I broke the last racket, I was happy. And then I realised, "F***, I don't have any more rackets." And I felt stupid.'

Venus Williams, who has won 8 grand slam titles, and who has her own clothing range,
on 'HOW TO BE STYLISH ON COURT' ...

Figure out what looks good for your body type: 'Not everyone can wear everything so you have to work out what works for you. If you don't find something that looks good on you, the joke is going to be on you.'

Wear what excites you: 'Tennis fashion has changed a lot in the last 10 or

15 years and has become more interesting. The future remains to be seen. Tennis is conservative, and tennis style is probably never going to be on the runways, but that doesn't mean it can't be exciting as well.'

Don't underestimate the importance of looking good on the court: 'Absolutely you will play better tennis if you feel good about what you're wearing. You will feel confident and you won't have to worry about what you're wearing and you can focus on your game. But if you don't feel good about what you're wearing, you will be constantly thinking, "I look terrible."'

Listen to your friends' opinions: 'Be willing to take some constructive criticism. Your real friends will help you out.'

Bethanie Mattek-Sands, who has been called the Lady Gaga of tennis, on 'HOW TO DRESS TO IMPRESS' ...

Be bold: 'It's a huge compliment that people call me the Lady Gaga of tennis. She has rocked some bizarre stuff. I would consider wearing a dress made out of meat, like Lady Gaga did, but it's tough to repeat something like that. Also, I need to be able to move and sweat on court, so I can't be as extreme as she is.'

Keep everyone guessing about what you're going to wear, and never wear the same thing twice: 'I wore a dress made out of tennis balls to a pre-Wimbledon party, and my husband thought I should wear it again, but you can't do that. The Wimbledon Museum have asked for it, but it's kind of special to me. I'm keeping it for now. People come to the house to try it on. The year that I wore knee-high socks at Wimbledon, the museum asked for those after the match, and I gave those to them. I was playing Venus Williams on Centre Court and I thought I was in trouble as an official came up to me and said: "Hey, we need to talk to you about your outfit." I thought I was about to get fined. There was real relief when they said, "Could you donate your outfit to the museum?"'

There's no harm in wearing things to win bets, or in just wearing the first thing you find in your suitcase: 'I once wore a cowboy hat on court. That was a dare by an ex-boyfriend. He didn't think I would do it. I was cut from my sponsor just before going to the Australian Open one year. I had all this stuff from the company with me and I was thinking, "I just got cut, I don't want to wear this," and so I had a dig around in my suitcase … and that's what I wore on court. I played in the hat and got fined for it. I'm not sure whether I would do that again – I was fined a thousand dollars. They said it was non-tennis attire. I've worn a lot of leopard-print stuff. I had a hot-pink leopard-print dress. I've worn a leopard print headband. My doubles partner, Sania Mirza, has said of my fashion sense, "No way could you pay me enough money to dress like Bethanie."'

Have fun with your fashion but don't let it distract you once the match starts: 'Once I'm on the court, I don't think about what I'm wearing. It's all business. I'm there to win a tennis match. Having fun with my outfits and my hair or tattoos, that's my personality, and it's relaxing. It gets my mind off the tennis, it's fun, and then I focus once I get on the court. Before going on court, I make sure that everything fits OK, and isn't going to restrict my movement or vision. You don't want to be worrying about that, as that would be a distraction. When I wore the cowboy hat, it was pinned on, so I could see everything.'

> **'I once wore a cowboy hat for a dare.'**
> **BETHANIE MATTEK-SANDS**

Ana Ivanovic, a former French Open champion and world No. 1, on 'HOW TO PACK YOUR RACKET BAG' …

Consider packing rackets strung at two different tensions: 'I usually carry about five rackets, strung at two different tensions: four at my regular tension and one tighter. I may change to a more tightly-strung racket depending on the conditions or if I feel my timing is a little off on that particular day. If the conditions are hot and the ball is flying quickly through the air, a tighter racket would be needed. But it's rare that I would change it mid-match, because I practise about 90 minutes before the match, so I know what conditions to expect. But conditions can change, and it's good to have that option.'

Pack a sports drink filled with electrolytes, and a banana, and some power bars. Avoid chocolate and fizzy drinks: 'A sports drink filled with electrolytes will keep you well hydrated. But you don't always have to buy a sports drink – I know they can be expensive. Instead, you could buy some electrolyte tablets or powder that you dissolve in water. A banana quickly releases energy, and power bars are also good to give you a boost of energy during a changeover. Avoid foods with high fat and sugar content, like chocolate. And fizzy drinks aren't good either, because they can cause you to become bloated: water is far better.'

Some players like to take lucky charms or mascots on court: 'In the past I carried lucky pennies.'

Don't forget a spare outfit and a towel: 'At professional tournaments, we can always ask the ball boys for a towel. But I would always recommend club players bring one of their own.'

Leave room in your bag for a book, string, stencils, ink, accessories, sunscreen, and lip balm: 'I don't like to unpack my racket bag too much, so I will often carry on to court some things that I won't actually use during a match. I will also carry my accessories: wristbands, visors and hair bands and hair ties. I actually don't leave anything in my locker: it's all in my bag.'

Pack the night before: 'I keep some of the stuff in there permanently until it runs out, for example the string, visors and shoes. But items like food and drinks I pack the night before, along with my clean tennis dress.'

Pat Rafter, a former world No. 1 and US Open champion,
on **'HOW TO BE SPORTING'** ...

If your ball toss hasn't come out right, and you catch the ball and you're keeping your opponent waiting, it's courteous to say sorry: 'It's not nice to have problems with your ball toss and get the yips. I was always embarrassed when I called out, "Sorry mate," but it's only polite to apologise.'

Don't feel as though you have to get in someone's face to win tennis matches: 'I have no problem with people getting excited and pumped up, but there's a line you shouldn't cross, even in big matches.'

While you shouldn't go out of your way to upset your opponent, that doesn't mean you should back down: 'I was right back in their face. I didn't mind a bit of a rumble.'

You can't change a player's nature – but you can teach them some manners: 'You've got to be careful if you've got a young player who is very excitable and gets pumped up, and you start telling him to tone it down. But you can persuade them to go about things in a more sporting way.'

Greg Rusedski, a former US Open finalist and world No. 4, on 'HOW TO ARGUE WITH AN UMPIRE' ...

Give them the Pete Sampras look to start off with: 'That's a frowny sort of look, which questions whether the umpire is being serious. What you're hoping is that if there's another close call, the umpire will feel a little bit worried.'

Keep testing the umpire: 'If you don't agree with a call, say "Are you sure?" That will keep the umpire thinking about their calls.'

An argument with an umpire can be tactical. Players sometimes have arguments with the umpire to psyche themselves up: 'They also do it to change the pace of the match. If they're losing, and the match is going against them, they want a stop in play so they will complain about a line-call just to change up the momentum.'

If you're concerned about saying too much to the umpire, and you want to control yourself, maybe focus on your racket strings, or turn your chair so you're facing away from the umpire: 'You don't want to be using any foul language with the umpire.'

You can yell. You have to release that anger and get it out of your system, as otherwise you're not going to play well. You're going to feel that there's an injustice there: 'Staying angry rarely helps you to play better tennis. The only player I've seen who has managed his anger, who has even been helped by his anger, is John McEnroe.'

Wimbledon referee Andrew Jarrett
on 'HOW TO DEAL WITH AN ANGRY PLAYER' ...

Treat the player as a responsible adult. Be honest and fair and listen carefully to what is being said: 'Ultimately, there are rules and sanctions and if you have to enforce them, you will. But hopefully it will be possible to go with a more humane approach first. Try common sense initially. In every rule book, I would suggest that rule number one is "use your common sense", and only then do you go into the detail.'

Be flexible: 'There are times to be tough. And there are also times to be a fatherly or brotherly type of figure. You're dealing with human beings, and everyone is going to react in a different way. There's not a hard and fast way of dealing with an angry tennis player.'

Always stay within the rules: 'You're trying to find a good solution for all concerned. But, from an officiating point of view, you have to find a solution that is within the rules of the sport. That's life, it can be good, bad or ugly.'

Mohamed Lahyani, who was in the chair for John Isner's
11-hour victory over Nicolas Mahut at the 2010 Wimbledon Championships,
on 'HOW TO BE A WORLD-CLASS UMPIRE' ...

Do not socialise with the players: 'We tend to stay in the same hotels as the players, so you will bump into them in the gym or in the lift or in the lobby, and we also take the same cars and buses out to the site. But there are strict rules about not socialising with the players, and especially not one-on-one. Of course, you say hello if you see them away from the courts, but if you had a drink with them in a bar, or a long conversation in a hotel corridor, I think that would look bad. By staying independent, you can make better decisions.'

Have a good breakfast, but do not drink too much coffee: 'You never know

whether you will have time to eat again during the day – I needed a good breakfast for that match at Wimbledon. I will also have a double espresso, but that will be my only coffee of the day. Many of the younger officials seem to think that coffee will keep them sharp, but if you drink too much of it you want to go to the bathroom all the time. If I had gone to the bathroom during that match at Wimbledon, keeping Mahut waiting for several minutes before he served to stay in the tournament yet again, and he had then got broken, I would have got the blame. After Isner had won, the first thing he said to me was: "How did you do that, sitting there in the chair all that time? What's your secret?"'

You must not drink alcohol within 12 hours of a match, and you can never have a drink if you are still at the tennis: 'Even if you're finished for the day, and the last match for the day has just gone on, it is forbidden to have a beer at the site, and I know some officials have lost their jobs over that.'

Do not go on court with any preconceived ideas: 'You know how some players are on court, as you have studied their personalities, but you have to start every match from scratch, and you must not think, "This guy has been a troublemaker in the past." You must be fair and treat everyone the same.'

We're all human and make mistakes, and if you admit to making an error, the players will have greater respect for you. Let angry players speak, and stay calm: 'Try to calm them down by engaging them in conversation during the changeovers, and by letting them talk, as they will want to have the last word. They want to let off steam, and you want them to feel comfortable on court.'

Players need to be confident and relaxed, and it's the same for umpires: 'If you're confident, you will make better decisions. If you're tense and nervous, the players will feel it.'

Concentration is key: 'I don't think people realise the pressure we are under as umpires, as the players are competing for so much prize money, and there are television cameras everywhere, with the microphones picking up everything you say, and the Hawk-Eye challenge system. If you lose your concentration for half a second and get something wrong, the whole world is going to know about it in half a second, and within ten minutes you're going to be on YouTube. During that match at Wimbledon, it felt as though every point was a match point.'

Dustin Brown, dreadlocked tennis player who defeated Lleyton Hewitt
in the second round of the Wimbledon Championships in 2013,
on 'HOW TO ENTERTAIN A CROWD' ...

If people see that you're having fun, they are going to enjoy watching you: 'I try to have as much fun as I can, and I guess people pick up on that.'

There will be nerves beforehand – it's the same for singers and actors before they go on stage – but once you step on court it's showtime: 'You have to get through those nerves as quickly as you can.'

Entertain the crowd, but the primary goal is to win the match: 'Entertaining people is a bonus.'

John Lloyd, a former British Davis Cup captain,
on 'HOW TO CAPTAIN A TENNIS TEAM' ...

You have to know what makes your players tick. It's as important for a captain to know his players' personalities as it is to know their games: 'You need harmony in the team. Tennis players are often very selfish – it's an individual sport, and you know how you want to prepare for a match, and how you want to play. So when you put individuals in a team, it's a very different dynamic. Putting certain characters together in doubles pairings is going to create friction, so you need to be clever about which players you put together.'

> 'I've been on teams with some odd people.'
> JOHN LLOYD

If a player is causing problems, and wrecking team spirit, don't be afraid to drop them: 'I've been on teams with some odd people before, and you just have to find a way of dealing with those people. But if a player is harming the team morale, that's different. You have to decide if you really want them to stay around.'

Radek Stepanek, who has won the Davis Cup with the Czech Republic,
on 'HOW TO BE PART OF A TENNIS TEAM' ...

Although some team conversations should remain confidential, it's always important to be honest, even if that honesty hurts: 'Probably someone doesn't want to hear it. But it's better to get it out there. If someone doesn't like it, I say that I don't care, and that I'm just expressing how I feel. And I will say to people that they can tell me their opinions. If you start with a clean table, you can get more done after that. Some opinions can be difficult but it's not always about being happy and relaxed and having fun. We have fun, but it's also serious as you're there to win. It's not about laughing, but about performing.'

You have to worry about others – for a tennis player, that's a big change: 'For me, that was a great thing as I love to be part of a team. I love the atmosphere. You're taking responsibility for the whole team. And in the Davis Cup you're taking responsibility for the country.'

To build team spirit, it's important to have dinner together. No one should have dinner on their own: 'That helps to bring the different personalities together. Maybe some guys are quiet and are happy in the corner, not talking too much. And there are other guys who like talking the whole time and doing some crazy stuff. You have to find some harmony between the people.'

Work hard. If the team gives everything and you still lose, at least you can say you tried your best: 'If you lose, it hurts. It always hurts. But if you can wake up in the morning and look in the mirror, and you know that you did everything in your power, then you can't do any more. When you lose in a situation like that, you shake your opponents' hands and say, "Well done." Then you wait for your next chance. But if you don't give everything, and you lose, that's going to kill you on the inside.'

Janko Tipsarevic, a former top 10 player,
on 'HOW TO USE THE HAWK-EYE CHALLENGE SYSTEM' ...

It's not smart to blow all your challenges immediately, just because you think you're right: 'Don't use them up too early. I always try to keep one challenge for the end of a set, especially when it's a tight match.'

Don't bother trying to use Hawk-Eye to get a breather or a mental break: 'I don't think the extra five seconds you get when Hawk-Eye looks at a line-call is going to give you enough of a break.'

Chris Kermode, Executive Chairman and President of the men's ATP World Tour, on 'HOW TO RUN A TENNIS TOURNAMENT' ...

You want to people think, if they're not there, they're missing out: 'That attracts everybody.'

If you start dictating to players what you think is right, you're going to start alienating people. Everyone wants to be listened to: 'Ultimately, you're going to have to make some decisions that won't appease everybody. But if you've gone through the process of listening, most of the time people are happy. Tennis players don't tend to be stupid. They might have a view, but if you speak to them and explain why you're doing what you're doing, 99 per cent of the time they understand.'

If players or spectators are unhappy, don't start hiding at the back of your office: 'You need to talk to people and to address the issue head on.'

There must be a social element to it: 'People are incredibly busy, and demands on people's time – work, family – are pretty intense, and there are so many different sporting and entertainment events which are trying to get your time and money. So the event has to be enjoyable and good value.'

Former Wimbledon head groundsman Eddie Seward on 'HOW TO HAVE A LAWN LIKE CENTRE COURT' ...

Work on the grass the whole year round: 'We cut it throughout the year. Many people make the mistake of letting out a big sigh of relief in September, and putting the mower in the shed for another year, and thinking that they don't need to cut their lawn again until the spring.'

Punch holes into the court to get some air into it: 'This allows the roots to develop in the autumn.'

If you're top-dressing the court with soil, you should do some analysis to make sure it's compatible with what's already there: 'You need to make sure it's the same soil all the way through.'

Scarify the lawn [rake out the moss and thatch] in the autumn: 'This is one thing that people often don't do – they think that it's going to cause a big mess. They are then making a bigger problem for themselves, as they are getting a lot of thatch, and the court becomes very soft and spongy and therefore the ball won't bounce very much.'

Keep urban foxes and pigeons away from the lawn: 'If a vixen gets on to the court and urinates, that kills the grass and kills the soil. Pigeons and other birds will eat the seeds, and the sulphur in their droppings will burn the grass a little bit. The ammonia in the droppings can also make your courts look like they have measles. At Wimbledon, we fly a hawk three times a week, which keeps pigeons away.'

INDEX